MW00777006

CHOOSE YOUR ENEMIES WISELY

CHOOSE YOUR ENEMIES WISELY

Business Planning for the Audacious Few

PATRICK BET-DAVID
WITH GREG DINKIN

PORTFOLIO | PENGUIN

Portfolio / Penguin
An imprint of Penguin Random House LLC
penguinrandomhouse.com

Most Portfolio books are available at a discount when purchased in quantity for sales
promotions or corporate use. Special editions, which include personalized covers, excerpts,
and corporate imprints, can be created when purchased in large quantities. For more information,
please call (212) 572-2232 or e-mail specialmarkets@penguinrandomhouse.com. Your local
bookstore can also assist with discounted bulk purchases using the Penguin Random House
corporate Business-to-Business program. For assistance in locating a participating retailer,
e-mail B2B@penguinrandomhouse.com.

Graphics by Valuetainment.

LIBRARY OF CONGRESS CATALOGING-IN-PUBLICATION DATA
Names: Bet-David, Patrick, author. | Dinkin, Greg, author.
Title: Choose your enemies wisely: business planning for
the audacious few / Patrick Bet-David, with Greg Dinkin.
Description: New York: Portfolio/Penguin, [2023]
Identifiers: LCCN 2023026548 (print) | LCCN 2023026549 (ebook) |
ISBN 9780593712849 (hardcover) | ISBN 9780593712856 (ebook)
Subjects: LCSH: Business planning. | Success in business.
Classification: LCC HD30.28 .B45845 2023 (print) | LCC HD30.28 (ebook) |
DDC 658.4/012—dc23/eng/20230707
LC record available at https://lccn.loc.gov/2023026548
LC ebook record available at https://lccn.loc.gov/2023026549

Printed in the United States of America
2nd Printing

Book design by Daniel Lagin

To all my past, current, and future enemies.
I'm thankful for you all!

YOU have no enemies, you say?
Alas! my friend, the boast is poor;
He who has mingled in the fray
Of duty, that the brave endure,
Must have made foes! If you have none,
Small is the work that you have done.
You've hit no traitor on the hip,
You've dashed no cup from perjured lip,
You've never turned the wrong to right,
You've been a coward in the fight.

Charles Mackay, Scottish author

Contents

PART THREE

Bringing Your Plan to Life

The Enemies Spoke

A wise man gets more use from his enemies than a fool from his friends.

Baltasar Gracián, seventeenth-century Spanish philosopher

I n December of 2002, I was twenty-four and broke, living with my dad in his small apartment. The only routine I had in my life was a rotating schedule of L.A. nightclubs that I went to six nights a week . . . Saddle Ranch, Garden of Eden, Century Club, Key Club, Palace, and Dublin's. Half the time, I only knew what night of the week it was because of the club I was in. Every week was the same, until I got kicked out of Dublin's for getting into too many fights.

Nothing was going well in my life. Things had gotten so bad that I had a discussion with an army recruiter about reenlisting. In return for wiping out $49,000 of debt, I would have to commit to six more years of service. I was days away from saying yes.

That year on Christmas Eve, with nothing else to do, I drove my dad to a relative's house for what should have been a fun break from my miserable life. When we arrived, the celebration was in full swing. Everyone was joking and laughing, and my dad started talking to some relatives in Assyrian. As I chatted with the other guests, I heard a guy who my dad had helped out years before make a sarcastic comment. He seemed amused at seeing how far my dad had fallen since he left Iran.

I remember hearing something like "Gabreal Bet-David, the brilliant chemist in Iran, now the ninety-nine-cent store cashier in America, twice divorced and still alone." The group of men around my dad had a good laugh. It was all true: my dad had been a brilliant chemist and now worked at a ninety-nine-cent store, where he was frequently robbed at gunpoint. Plus, he really had gotten divorced twice from the same woman, my mom. Even though this guy didn't have any ill intentions, I could see on my dad's face that it hurt. He looked smaller to me.

Something about that man laughing at my dad—and maybe more important, the look of shame on my dad's face—produced a fury in me that I had never felt before. I was intense back then, but this brought out another level of rage. Instead of taking a swing at the guy, I walked right up to the circle of men and said, "Nobody talks to my dad like that. For all the things he's done for you, you're not going to talk to him that way. This is not going to happen. We're out of here."

I turned to my dad, and repeated, "We're out of here." He didn't move. Maybe it was the pride of not wanting to show his hurt, but he dug in. The room got silent. I'm nine inches taller than my dad, but he was still my dad, and I would never disrespect him. Somehow, I managed to control myself, and as calmly as I could, I said, "Dad, I'm your ride. We're leaving."

The men were staring at us—father and son locked in a silent battle. It was a tense moment. If the wrong thing had been said, it could have turned ugly. With all eyes in the room glued to us, my dad made a comment about wanting to beat traffic. It allowed him to save face so we could leave the party, but I could tell that he was livid.

We walked out, and my dad managed to hold his tongue until we got to the car. He turned to me, eyes blazing, and said, "What is wrong with you, son? You just embarrassed me in front of my family. This is not how you handle yourself. The guy was just kidding. He didn't mean anything by it."

"I don't care whether it's a joke or if he's being serious," I said. "No one talks to you that way." For thirty minutes, I couldn't stop repeating to my dad, "*They may have to kill me, but the world is going to know your last name.*" I couldn't even tell you who "they" referred to, but I was going ballistic. For thirty minutes, I couldn't stop repeating, "They may have to kill me, but the world is going to know your last name."

In response, my dad just kept shaking his head, saying, "What is wrong with you, son?" I can't tell you what my dad was thinking at the time, but I could sense that he didn't really believe me. I had yet to prove that I could stick with my goals, so I'm sure he thought that I lacked the discipline to back up my words. To him, it must have sounded more like a tantrum than a declaration.

That didn't stop me from carrying on. "No one talks to my dad like this. Nobody does. And you shouldn't let anybody talk to you like this. No matter how hard a life we've had."

We arrived at our run-down complex in Granada Hills and went up to the apartment we shared. I had one final thing to say to my dad: "I'm going to show the world how special a father you have been." Then I called my sister and brother-in-law and told them to come over the next day for a meeting. When they arrived, we all sat down, and I said, "I'm not going to sleep until the world knows our last name, Bet-David. It's game over."

—

The holiday party happened more than six years before I started my financial services firm and more than a decade before I started making content for Valuetainment, my media company. So what does my dad being insulted have to do with business planning?

Everything.

As you will soon understand, **the most critical element for success in business planning is choosing your enemies wisely.** Yes, you heard that right—enemies. In business, you will face challenges, haters, betrayals, bankruptcies, and ideologies that stand in the way of your success. But what if I told you that these so-called enemies could become your greatest source of fuel? What if you could turn shame, guilt, anger, disappointment, and heartbreak into the fire that propels you toward your wildest dreams?

You're going to see how to leverage your enemies to light a fuse that ignites your power to transform. We'll dive deep into the mindset of successful entrepreneurs who have turned their greatest challenges into their biggest strengths. You'll learn how to harness the energy of emotions and use them as a catalyst for success. But this is not just a book about mindset. I'll also provide you with practical tools and strategies to help you navigate the challenges of business. You will see how to use the fuel from your enemies to **create a business plan that is emotional, logical, and actionable.**

The night of the party, I had no clue what a gift this condescending relative had given to me. I didn't realize that, to find the key to my success, exactly what I needed was someone to insult my last name and my father. I learned that I do better fighting for others than for myself. All I needed was for someone to piss me off by offending my dad.

The man who insulted my dad created a fire that would move me in ways that I didn't know I could be moved. It's no coincidence that this party was right after my dad had another heart attack and stayed at UCLA Medical Center for a month. It intensified my fear of him dying without meeting his future grandkids. I wanted my kids to know him because I had never met his dad, my grandfather. When many bad things happen at once and we can no longer handle the stress, we have either a breakdown or a breakthrough. By the grace of God, I found a way to channel all this adversity into changing my life.

With the goal of showing the world what the Bet-David name is all about, I immediately dropped all bad habits. I was done with clubs. With my free time, all I did was read books on investments, sales, and anything that had to do with business. My sister and my friend Robby recommended *How to Win Friends and Influence People* and *How to Master the Art of Selling.* I took notes and read them over and over.

My business did not take off the next day, much less the next year. The last thing I want you to think is that my path was easy. Obstacles will appear for you, as they did for me. Right when you start to make progress, you'll lose a big customer, or your top sales rep will get poached. For me, those challenges seemed to show up on days the bill collectors gave me an ultimatum. It made it harder to resist the military recruiter, who was there to solve all my problems by promising to wipe out my debt and provide an easy way out.

You're going to face the same type of resistance. It's going to take something extra to fight through the adversity. Just when I thought I had turned a corner, I lost a big sale, and my only asset in life—a black Ford Expedition that my friends called "Big Mama"—got repo'd. It felt like one step forward and three steps back, and it almost drained my energy when all my effort wasn't showing up in my bank account.

Whenever things got really tough for me, I could always go back to the image of those men making my dad feel small. The desire to prove them wrong was stronger than the urge to quit. That's why I'm going to keep emphasizing the importance of having enemies.

Twenty-one years after that holiday party, this book was published. What I want you to know is that sometimes we spend so much time trying to find *how* to win at life that we miss the entire point. Maybe you need to look for *why* to win in life. Did somebody humiliate you? Did somebody manipulate you? Is there a teacher or family member who made you feel ashamed? We're all driven in different ways, but **the right enemy can drive you in ways an ally never can.**

When "experts" say that you shouldn't get emotional in business, I ask what kind of success they've had. They rattle off their degrees and publications and brag about their prestigious universities and privileged upbringing. Most of the time, they don't have any business success to speak of. Maybe nobody offended them in life or maybe they were taught to keep that emotion bottled up and not bring it into business. No matter the reason, when I see that they don't have enemies to fuel them, I realize that I am the privileged one.

ENEMIES: THE MISSING ELEMENT OF STANDARD BUSINESS PLANNING

Most people love to *hear* a rags-to-riches story. There's another group of people—like you, the audacious few—who want the formula to *create their own*. Words like "perseverance" and "heart" are great, but they fail to tell you exactly what to do to fulfill your own dream.

You may know my background and how I went from nothing (fled Iran at age ten during the Iran-Iraq War, divorced parents, on welfare, 1.8 GPA, no college options) to starting my own financial services firm at age thirty. In July of 2022, I sold the business to focus on my next twenty-year run. Valuetainment, a YouTube channel I started to offer business advice I wish I'd had when I was starting out, became the most popular channel for entrepreneurs. It all happened while I was running another company. This allowed me to later leverage the brand to build a full-scale media, consulting, and production company. In just a few years, Valuetainment has produced the number one business podcast on Spotify, hosted live conferences, grown to just shy of a hundred employees, and mentored entrepreneurs to massively scale their businesses.

The question I think you want answered is, *How?*

Did I have a secret? Did I reach into my vault and pull out a revolutionary idea that had never been seen before in a boardroom?

No . . . and yes.

No, because I started with the same old business plan that everyone uses.

Yes, because year after year, after reviewing what succeeded and what failed, I kept adapting. I created a radically different approach to a common business practice that made all the difference in the world.

I created a one-of-a-kind business plan.

In all my research, it was unlike any business plan I had ever seen. It took years of testing and countless revisions to figure out the exact formula. It then took a couple more years to simplify it so anyone could benefit from it. What I'm most proud of is that it's duplicatable. Anyone, and most importantly, YOU can create this plan.

I used logic and thought strategically. That's where most people start. It's also where most people stop. I wasn't interested in going through the motions to create an unexciting business in which money was the only measuring stick. I wanted something magical that would inspire me and my team.

I chose my enemies wisely, because they gave me the energy to keep pursuing the plan long after I had more money than I would ever need. Now that I've "made it"—at least in some people's eyes—slowing down isn't even a thought. Instead, I've graduated to new enemies who create the fuel that keeps me more excited and committed than ever.

Using this business plan, my financial services business grew from sixty-six agents to forty thousand agents in thirteen years and a multi-nine-figure exit. Most of the agents don't have college degrees, and dozens are million-dollar-plus earners. There are also the thousands of people in other industries who I've coached on business plans that have scaled companies and achieved unprecedented success.

There's a reason I called out the "audacious few" in the subtitle. This book is for visionaries, dreamers, and psycho-competitors. I can see how some might think my approach is extreme. But in my view, you have to be "extreme" to be part of the audacious few.

If you want to gain every edge possible, if you are honest and receptive to feedback, I'll guide you down a path that leads to extraordinary results. If you are a competitive person who thrives on doubters and haters, you want to know your blind spots so you can get better. You may be one of the few people who, **when it comes to your life, legacy, and family, refuse to take shortcuts or play small**.

WHAT YOU WILL GAIN FROM THIS BOOK

Where you are now in your career doesn't matter. Whether you are in the C-suite, own a business, work as a solopreneur or sales rep, or are an employee or a student thinking about starting a business, the process is the same. I'll show you how to choose an enemy and leverage that emotion to build the right business plan.

I've seen people who were down and out, who had stopped dreaming, find their way back and go on to achieve incredible things. It started with choosing the right enemy. It's the first and most critical element to writing an effective business plan.

I wrote this book because it can change the game for entrepreneurs and intrapreneurs (people who work for a company and operate with an entrepreneurial mindset)—whether you are hoping to become one or already running a big or small business. Since other plans fail, we're going down a much different path. This is not the boring approach that most people teach. If you're looking to cure insomnia, you can go buy any course on how to write a business plan. What you'll learn here is how to become a leader who lifts up your family, friends, and team.

This process of writing a business plan is unlike anything you've ever done before.

For the longest time, I hated writing business plans. It felt like homework assigned by my least favorite teacher. I didn't have the attention span or the education to get through a technical book on business planning. I needed to figure out how to organize my ideas and create a tactical plan for my business. At the same time, I wanted to connect to my heart and write something that inspired me. I've learned that writing an effective business plan only requires three things:

1. It must be simple enough for you to want to write it.
2. It must have emotion that is fueled by enemies.
3. It must have logical steps that are clear and well organized.

Writing a business planning happens at different times, so it doesn't matter when you are reading this book. You may be starting a business, reorganizing your existing business, or setting new goals. Others of you may be about to begin a new sports season or a new academic year. The time horizon doesn't matter. In fact, this approach is also perfect for a fundraising or political campaign. What all these situations have in common is that you are looking forward and feeling hopeful. There's nothing like a clean slate, a fresh start, an undefeated record. There are no wrongs to right and no fires to put out. This allows you to put all the pieces in place to make your goals a reality.

The plan works for people at every level of business:

- Complete beginners, without college degrees, just starting out in business
- CEOs doing half a billion in revenue, who want to scale or plan an exit

- Seasoned executives who want to become intrapreneurs and increase their net worth
- Veterans, straight out of the military, starting careers in sales or as entrepreneurs
- Sales leaders who want to grow revenue and motivate their team
- Couples who work in a business together and want financial and family success

Choosing your enemies is the catalyst. If done correctly, it's the rocket fuel that gets you going.. Acting on revenge and envy leads some people to choose the wrong enemy. That type of emotion can end up destroying you. **The key is to choose your enemies wisely.** As you will see, there's a process to it. You must identify the right target and get emotional when you think about why you must defeat this enemy. You'll see many examples to understand why this is so effective, so you can do it yourself.

You also need a methodical plan. You may have heard that people must know why before you can tell them how. A more accurate statement is that you and those around you must know *both* your why and your how.

I've taught my team how to direct their energy into choosing the right enemy, and I've "trained the trainer" to teach business planning to everyone in the company. That's why I know it can be duplicated, and why you can both learn it for yourself and teach it to your team.

I believe that all dreams are sacred. For entrepreneurs, there's even more risk and uncertainty. Many of you have walked away from high-paying jobs to risk your reputation and livelihood on a dream. In these moments, full of hope, you begin to author your own destiny. I know that what happens next will determine your next year and shape your legacy. I also know that poor planning is why most dreams die.

That can all change now as long as you put in the effort to follow the step-by-step guide for how to build a business plan. As you go through the steps, you will

- learn how to tap into your emotion and channel it to become relentless;
- identify your vision, define who you want to be, and uncover your craziest dreams;
- know the specific action steps to take to accomplish your Big Hairy Audacious Goals (BHAGs);
- learn best practices to secure investors and raise capital;
- improve your relationships, both inside and outside your business;
- master how to lead your team so they are as inspired as you are.

You'll finish this book and never look at a business plan the same. What you are about to learn I have taught my teams for fifteen years. If it only worked for me, you could argue that it's not duplicatable. The fact that it has worked for thousands of other leaders is why I know it will work for you—if you put in the effort.

Once and for all, you will have a complete guide to walk you through how to make your business and your life succeed.

And it all starts with the one step you absolutely cannot miss.

You must choose your enemies wisely.

PART ONE

Integrating Logic and Emotion to Build Your Plan

CHAPTER 1

The 12 Building Blocks

The general who wins the battle makes many calculations in his temple before the battle is fought. The general who loses makes but few calculations beforehand.

Sun Tzu

I was working on a massive deal. Millions of dollars were on the line, and I needed to focus. I told my assistant to hold all calls and tackle anyone who tried to walk through my door. In retrospect, I should have hired a bigger assistant. Actually, I don't think even Lawrence Taylor, in his prime, could have stopped this guy.

He stormed into my office and screamed, "I'm so sick of my life!" He was shaking. "I can't live like this anymore. I've got nowhere to go and nowhere else to turn. I want to win so bad. I'm telling you, right now, that I'm going to be the best agent in this office! Nothing can stop me!"

His rage turned to sadness, and for thirty minutes the tears didn't stop. Ernie was nineteen at the time. He had four hundred dollars to his name, a high school degree, and no business skills. Ernie had all the desire in the world, but I wondered if it would be enough for him to compete.

Earlier that day, Larry had presented his business plan. He displayed all the polish and professionalism that you would expect from a UCLA graduate who had worked at Northrop Grumman. His words were as crisp as his starched shirt. His parents had taught him well, and if he ever needed help, they were there to provide a safety net.

As you might expect, Larry's business plan was impeccable. It was full of Excel spreadsheets and charts and clearly mapped-out goals for the year. When I asked him to share with me why his business was so important to him, he looked confused. When I asked Larry about his enemies, he pointed to the plan, which was bound, and said, "All the relevant details are included herein, sir." I seriously thought about checking Larry for a pulse.

Ernie's plan was a mess, and that's being generous. There was no structure to it and no numbers or projections. There weren't even any bullet points. When I asked him about his strategy for prospecting, Ernie broke down again. He said he was tired of the poverty and drama that came with being in a family affected by alcoholism. "Ernie," I said, "I understand what you're going through, but you still need a plan. What is it that you actually want to do?"

He couldn't find any words. I could see the toll that his family life had taken on him even before I knew much of his story. It took Ernie several minutes to pull himself together enough so that he could speak. Finally, he managed to mutter, "I'll do whatever it takes not to be poor."

If Ernie had been in the room for Larry's presentation, I wonder if he would have been so bold in his claim to be number one. But I saw something in him that I recognized in myself. Unlike some other business leaders, I viewed emotion in a positive light.

If you were in my shoes at the time, who would you have chosen to work with: Ernie or Larry? You don't know these two people, but you know their type. In fact, they represent thousands of people I've worked with over the years. Just about everyone I've met—before they evolved into the audacious few—fell into one of two types: logic or emotion. To make them easy to remember, Larry represents logic and Ernie represents emotion.

In 2005, when we sat down in my Granada Hills office, they were both dreaming of entrepreneurial success.

Based on what you know about these two guys, who would you bet on to succeed in achieving their goals, whether they are losing weight, starting a business, or moving up the ranks in a company?

Your answer to these questions will tell me a lot about you. If you're more in your head, you'll bet on Larry. If you're more in your heart, you'll bet on Ernie.

What I've learned over two decades is that neither Larry nor Ernie is a smart bet to accomplish his goals. The logical people are right to believe that Ernie won't be able to stay organized long enough to get the job done, much less raise capital. The emotional people are right to wonder what's going to keep Larry motivated. If you think like me, you would be asking Ernie, "If you've identified poverty as your enemy and are so determined to defeat it, why *don't* you have a plan?"

Here's where this gets interesting. You might think that Ernie has the advantage because he's got more to play for. He's more motivated because he *needs* it more. On the surface, you would be right. But what I've uncovered from doing thousands of plans with people is that Larry can *find* a reason to want it more. We all have a heart. We all have wounds and dreams that make us emotional. Most people in business have been trained not to go there. For some, they have made it a point to avoid emotion in order to stay centered. For others, they have suffered so much heartache that they focus on protecting themselves from getting hurt.

You can probably guess what question I ask that creates the most emotion in people. *Who are your enemies?* If they don't answer right away, I ask who their haters are, who has doubted them or stood in their way, and who they need to prove wrong. Oftentimes I get blank stares. When I dig a little deeper (I'll sit in silence as long as I need to—never underestimate the power of silence), the answer usually comes. The emotion that had been bottled up spills out. Maybe Larry still has scars from being laughed at in gym class for being the chubby kid who couldn't climb a rope. Maybe his gym teacher haunts his dreams. It could be an old boss, his more successful friend, or a family member that moves him emotionally. Before we can move forward, we must know the enemy.

WHAT MATTERS MORE: EXPERIENCE OR DRIVE?

Let's continue to compare emotional and logical people. Would you bet on a polished salesman who was trained by Oracle and had plenty of savings, or a rookie rep with no skills who needed that sale to feed his family?

Would you bet on a desperate systems engineer who is in debt to his bookie or a happy, experienced engineer to finish your new app on a tight deadline?

Would you bet on the team that is more experienced and better *prepared* or the team that is *possessed*? By "possessed" I mean that it could be that they have a chip on their shoulder, are mourning the loss of a player, or have a deep sense of pride.

I hope what you're saying is, "Enough of the examples of comparing logic to emotion, Pat. Why can't it be both?"

Not only can it be both, **your business plan must be both emotional and logical**. That's why I want you to see which side you favor, and where you need to improve. If you're only logical, you have probably struggled to inspire people. With my approach, you will know what you need to change to accomplish that. If you're only emotional, you have struggled to develop systems and stay organized. This is why you'll benefit from the structure of a methodical plan.

There's one other thing to keep in mind. As much as I value emotion, there is also a downside. A person willing to do anything to win often *will do anything* to win—including break laws (and limbs). If they work with you, as an employee, contractor, or vendor, they could put your business at risk. This is another reminder that it's the *right type of emotion* that you're seeking, in others and in yourself, to fuel your plan.

Before we continue, it's important to clarify what emotion is *not* and what it *is* in the context of business planning.

Emotion is *not* impulsive, irrational, melodramatic, temperamental, or hot-blooded.

Emotion *is* passionate, obsessed, maniacal, relentless, powerful, and purposeful.

The words for what emotion is *not* describe the people who have chosen the wrong enemy. The list of words for what emotion *is* describe the audacious few who become unstoppable.

The missing link in business planning—as well as business meetings, presentations, pitches, and recruiting—**is integrating emotion and logic.**

Do I sound like a broken record yet? Good. I've learned from decades of leading people and making more mistakes than I'd like to remember that repetition is key. Because it's been so deeply ingrained in most of us to separate emotion and logic, I will continue to emphasize that the plan has to *move you*. And it has to tell you exactly what levers must get pushed and when.

Just about every business plan written by a Larry or an Ernie fails. One or the other is not enough.

One of the barriers to using this plan is the belief that there's no place for emotion in business. There's also a belief that there's no place for crying in sports, but the man most famous for crying in football, Coach Dick Vermeil, was inducted into the Pro Football Hall of Fame and is the only head coach to win both the Super Bowl and the Rose Bowl. Michael Jordan, Serena Williams, Conor McGregor, and Tiger Woods are all emotional. They may display that emotion differently, but they are emotional.

The same goes for business leaders. Elon Musk is similar to two other business leaders I respect, the late Andy Grove and the late Steve Jobs, because they embraced emotion in business. They were also master strategists who could channel their emotion into logical steps.

Being enthusiastic isn't enough. It's also not enough to create the most brilliant spreadsheets. Being part of the audacious few means that you embrace integrating emotion and logic.

6 Ways People Treat Business Plans

1. Don't do it at all.
2. Treat it as homework: go through the motions.
3. Half-ass it to impress others.
4. Outline a thorough plan that's only logical.
5. Describe an emotional dream without any logical steps.

The only way that works . . .

6. **Fueled by an enemy and combining emotion and logic.**

HOW I RAISED $10 MILLION BY INTEGRATING EMOTION AND LOGIC

When I first started my financial services firm in 2009, I was full of emotion. I would tell anyone who would listen that we would have five hundred thousand licensed agents by 2029. For some people, it was easy to dismiss a cocky thirty-year-old who had never started a business before. Others were inspired by my passion and asked the next logical question: *How* will you reach five hundred thousand licensed agents?

In other words, I successfully used the emotion from having a big vision to grab their attention. I made them want to know more. This is an important skill. But when it came to the *how*, I continued with emotion. "We're going to have a sick culture! We will have ridiculous grit. We're going to create amazing events."

If you love words, you'll notice how many adjectives I used. As they were in this case, adjectives are often a poor substitute for a concrete strategy. Without a logical plan, no serious investor was interested.

My story mirrors that of many entrepreneurs. The ability to move people emotionally is a rare quality that allows a select few to start a company and convince others to follow them without any proof. Intrapreneurs, consultants, and accountants tend to be strong where entrepreneurs are weak. They're great with financial projections and tactical plans. That's why business partnerships that check both the emotional and logical boxes are so effective. Steve Jobs/Steve Wozniak, Warren Buffett/Charlie Munger, Mark Zuckerberg/Sheryl Sandberg, and Bill Gates/Paul Allen (and later, Bill Gates/Steve Ballmer) are excellent examples of balanced business partnerships.

I didn't have a cofounder, and it wasn't until later that I developed logical skills and recruited logical team members to complement my strengths. When I first started my firm, I was a lone wolf who only possessed some of the building blocks.

Fast forward to 2017, when I wanted to raise $10 million for the business. My vision hadn't changed. I would still tell anyone who would listen that we would have five hundred thousand licensed agents by 2029. But this time, when an investor asked how, I had a very logical answer. A big reason was that I had hired Tom Ellsworth, a logical and experienced strategist who understood the game of raising capital, to be our president. Tom had played a key role in several exits, including JAMDAT, which was acquired for $680 million by EA Sports.

With Tom by my side, we put together a pitch deck and financial projections. In chapter 9, you'll see the exact formula. Our pitch to investors included our growth rate over the previous eight years, projections for future growth based on real data, a specific growth plan with tactical strategies, and metrics that compared us to others in our industry.

A passionate presentation *and* coherent plans and projections were included in the pitch. Both emotion and logic are required to motivate investors.

They couldn't write the check for $10 million fast enough. That's the power of integrating emotion and logic.

2 Types of Stories to Tell

STORIES THAT INSPIRE AND INVITE (EMOTIONAL)

Get others excited

STORIES THAT VALIDATE YOUR POINT (LOGICAL)

Get others focused

WINNERS IN ALL FIELDS INTEGRATE EMOTION AND LOGIC

Once you start working through this plan, you will see how emotion and logic complement each other. I know most of us can access both, even though we've been trained to rely on one or the other. A clue that reminded me that I had the ability to use logic was that as a kid, I spent hours studying baseball box scores. Numbers made sense to me. I just didn't have the experience to bring analytics into my business. After I read the book *Moneyball* (and later watched the film where Brad Pitt played Billy Beane), all I could talk about was data. I learned to love gathering data and dissecting business analytics.

It doesn't mean that I stopped being emotional. I constantly pour my heart out to my team, and I know that when I touch their hearts, then (and only then) can I get into the details of how to execute. If I talk about *what* to do before I talk about *why* to do it, I lose people.

I've made every mistake possible when creating business plans, but I learned a valuable lesson from each one. You must begin by choosing an enemy and then combine emotion and logic every step of the way. Emotion reminds us *why* we do it. Logic tells us *how* to do it.

You know how I know you're going to love integrating emotion and logic? Because it resonates with people from all backgrounds regardless of personality, temperament, and education. I've seen the following types of people thrive when they started using all the building blocks:

1. Accountants, COOs, and analytical types, because they finally understand why people fall asleep during their "brilliant" logical presentations—and why no one had the fire to execute strategies that made sense but didn't *move* people.

2. The women leaders in my financial services company (55 percent of the firm versus 17 percent industry-wide), because after hearing their whole careers that there was no place for emotion in business, they thrived when hearing from their CEO the importance of expressing emotion.

3. The minority leaders in our company (54 percent Latino, 24 percent Black), because they came to view their underdog status and having a chip on their shoulder as an asset.

4. Former military members, because they resonate with the emotion of fighting for your country based on pride as well as the logic of having a tactical plan.

5. Former athletes, because the best coaches in sports are masters at blending logic and emotion. Pregame talks that create emotion are legendary for motivating athletes to exceed their potential. Yet they only work when there is a logical game plan that goes with it.

Whether it's in sports, war, or business, you can have a team ready to run through walls for you, but they need to know *which* walls and *how* to run through them.

THE TEAM THAT WINS IN SPORTS HAS THE BEST

Game plan

THE MILITARY UNIT THAT WINS IN BATTLE HAS THE BEST

Tactical plan

THE BUSINESS THAT BUILDS THE MOST LONG-TERM VALUE HAS THE BEST

Business plan

Logic is as equally important as emotion. In fact, it's 50 percent of the foundation of this book and what led me to create the 12 Building Blocks.

These building blocks integrate emotion and logic in a seamless way. Let's take a look at them in the following graphic:

When you look at this chart, I want you to focus on three things. First, choosing your enemy is the foundation. You must start there in order to fuel yourself to put in the work and sacrifice that's required to succeed. Next, you'll see that there are six emotional and six logical building blocks that you will integrate throughout the plan.

The last thing to notice is that the only way to reach the top and be part of the audacious few is to complete all 12 Building Blocks.

The 12 Building Blocks are:

Enemy and Competition

Will and Skill

Mission and Plan

Dreams and Systems

Culture and Team

Vision and Capital

Because emotion and logic are intertwined, each chapter will blend an emotional block and a logical block. To create the business plan that will take you to the next level, you will fill out every block, even if it's only a few sentences. Each chapter has action items, thought experiments, and questions to guide you through filling out the blocks and writing your best business plan ever.

While you are filling in the building blocks, keep in mind that you are writing your business plan for three different audiences:

1. **You.** You've got to be lit up by it and clear on your actions.
2. **Your team.** A strong plan will get your team on the same page to clarify the mission, act with both purpose and urgency, and operate efficiently.
3. **Investors.** What you share with investors will be very different from what you do for yourself and your team. In chapter 9, you will see how investors look at your business—and what they need to see to write you a big check.

LARRY AND ERNIE LEARNED TO INTEGRATE

Remember the person I met in 2005 who we called Ernie? He struggled at first because he lacked skills and experience. His work ethic was enough to keep him in the game for a few years, but he refused to read books or address his weaknesses. He said he was *willing* to do anything, but what that really meant was that he would work hard in areas that were in his comfort zone. In truth, he wasn't *capable* of doing much of anything. He nearly dropped out of the business.

The other guy I met in 2005, who we called Larry, came out of the gate strong. He was competent, organized, and met his deadlines. Because of his reliability, he got hired full-time and started moving up the ranks. But just as Ernie was faltering, Larry was plateauing. He had bought a house, got married, and proved he could make it. He was smart enough to be able to coast and get his job done, which is what he did. Before long, he was a card-carrying member of what I call the 4:59 club, the underachievers who are so anxious to leave work that they can't even wait for the clock to strike five o'clock. Without knowing his enemies or connecting to his emotions, Larry's outlets became fantasy football, darts, and craft beer. Because Ernie had more drive, he didn't arrive at the bar until seven, but he was right there with Larry shutting it down.

They both needed what the other had. Half of the building blocks were not enough to do their jobs, much less accomplish their dreams. Larry was as allergic to what he called "touchy-feely stuff" as Ernie was to spreadsheets and books. As is the sad case for most of us, they weren't willing to change until adversity struck.

Larry's wife threatened to leave him. Ernie's direct boss gave him sixty days to bring his skill set up to industry standards. Finally faced with the harsh reality of their shortcomings, they were forced to make a decision: give up or find a way to change.

I'm humbled that they both came to me for help. When I presented the framework for this business plan to each of them, the one you have in your hands now, they both felt a ray of hope. Their task was defined. All they had to do was fill in twelve blocks. That's not to say that it was easy, but it was definitely simple. In fact, being faced with blank blocks on a piece of paper forced them to confront their weaknesses and identify solutions. Ernie's skill gap was obvious. When he filled in that block with the courses he was going to take and the books he was going to read, he gained momentum. For Larry, who had never really considered his vision or his enemies, he had to dig deeper to understand what really drove him and what he wanted life to look like for his family over the next two decades. He went from being directionless to having a clear mission.

You are likely at a place in your career where you know what has already created success and what's holding you back from more. The challenge is knowing how to leverage your superpowers while addressing your shortcomings. If it gives you peace of mind, I've sat down with thousands of people who were in a similar place. Once they saw how simple, actionable, and effective this plan is, they naturally integrated emotion and logic and achieved incredible results. I can point to thousands of regular people who soared by using this approach.

After reading this chapter, I hope you have the same level of urgency as I did after leaving that Christmas party. You're so inspired that you want to take over the world. That's what emotion is supposed to do: get you to act. It's also why you need logic to step in. Just as you wouldn't get married when you were drunk (on alcohol or infatuation), you wouldn't invest your life savings without the proper due diligence. That's why before we move forward with the first building block, choosing the right enemy, we must first look back.

CHAPTER 2

Look Back to Create Duration, Depth, and Magic

The farther back you can look, the farther forward you are likely to see.

Winston Churchill

can't tell you how many times I've recommended the book *The 5 Love Languages*. I even made a video called "The 9 Love Languages of Entrepreneurs" because it's so important to understand what makes people tick. I also know that everyone is different. It's the rare individual who takes the time to understand the different love languages (or, in business terms, behavior/buyer styles) of everyone they meet.

The person who recommended *The 5 Love Languages* to me conducted an interesting survey. He asked every divorced person he knew what their ex's love language was. Almost none of them had a clue. Imagine being married to someone and not knowing what makes them feel loved and appreciated. Is it any wonder they got divorced?

What all these failed marriages have in common is that they *failed to plan*.

Some mistakes seem so obvious. When we watch Dr. Phil question someone who made an illogical choice, we find ourselves asking the same question as the TV host: "What *were* you thinking?" Logic was nowhere to be found. These people were acting solely on emotion. They were unbalanced. They had never considered any of the logical building blocks. There are so many case studies of failed businesses that anyone with the slightest amount of logic would have known were dead on arrival. But most people whose businesses failed missed one crucial step that could have changed their fate.

They only looked forward. Before you write a business plan, **you must first look back**.

Before writing any plan, this is a can't-miss step. Let's think about the process of going through a breakup. After it happens, some of us can't wait to just go to a bar (or swipe right!) and meet someone new. We say we're moving on. Then that one doesn't work, and then the next one. And the next one. Four years go by, and we say, "Wait a minute. How come I don't have a steady relationship? How come none of these things are working out?" I see the same pattern for far too many entrepreneurs.

Whether it's dating or business, there's a simple explanation. An important question was not asked: *What should I have done differently?* You either avoided seeing your role in the problem or you rationalized your role. You didn't bother looking at trends or searching for your own weaknesses. In short, you failed to see *yourself* as the common denominator.

Some people believe that it's best to look forward and forget about the past. They argue that there's something to be said for setting the scoreboard back to zero. If you've sold your house and are moving into a new one, there's no reason to worry about how you let the garage get so messy or the closets so cluttered. Or is there?

First off, unless this is your very first business venture, there is never really a clean slate. The residue is always you! Your habits are what created the messy garage and cluttered closets. You'd better take the time to understand *why* it happened. Is there a trend that you keep picking up on that you know, deep down, is not effective and is not working for you?

I'm emphasizing this point because I missed it for so many years. It took a lot of failure for me to understand that the *most important data for you is found in the year that just passed.*

In order to predict the future, you have to study history.

What happened last year for you? What went right? Judge your year based on what percentage of your goals became a reality. If you hit 100 percent of your goals, that might be an indication that that your goals weren't challenging enough. Instead of setting goals that forced you to stretch, you chose ones that were easy to attain. It's often a sign of not picking the right enemy. Once you identify who you need to beat, you will naturally raise the standard for what you must achieve.

If you achieved less than 60 percent of your goals, it tells me one of two things. One, you didn't give the best effort, or two, you didn't have the best strategy in place. So it's effort or strategy. In my experience, most of the time it's number one, effort. In these cases, emotion is lacking because the right enemy wasn't chosen.

A lot of people love to give excuses. They'll say that no one understands what's unique about their business and their hardships. They'll complain about the market. They'll complain about anything.

Many people make the same mistake when it comes to business plans. They are so anxious to forget about the previous year and wash it away. They comfort themselves with the idea of a clean slate and a fresh start.

You may be excited about a new relationship, but unless you examine what went wrong with the previous three relationships—the trends, your blind spots, etc.—you're going to keep making the same mistakes.

If you want to skip this part, if you want to do everything you can to forget about last year—that means you need it the most. When there's one person insisting that there's no reason to do an autopsy on his rich grandmother, that's the guy I suspect of foul play!

Every now and then, when a football team plays a terrible game, the coach will throw out the film and forget about it. But most of the time, especially if you have a coach like Bill Belichick or Nick Saban, they're going to go through every play in excruciating detail. If a software launch goes badly, the project manager will do a postmortem on every step of the process. The same goes for a heart surgeon.

Looking back to learn from mistakes is a linchpin of military training. Every operation requires a debriefing. Information about what went right and what went wrong must get disseminated in order for best practices to become part of new operating procedures.

A business is no different. How are you going to fix problems if you haven't deconstructed the process and figured out where things went wrong? There's an entire book called *Debrief to Win*, written by Robert "Cujo" Teschner, a former Air Force Top Gun, to show businesses how to study the past. According to Teschner, "the key to an organization's long-term success is its practice of accountability and the degree to which its leaders hold themselves and their teams accountable for the decisions they make."

Do you practice this type of accountability? Do you have the courage and patience to sit down with your team and discuss the specific details about what went wrong? I can tell you that if you're building a business, you're going to make plenty of bad decisions. You are definitely going to make a lot of bad hires. If not, you'll be a business of one! There's nothing wrong with making mistakes.

New mistakes are okay. Old mistakes are not.

When you make a bad hire, don't just have your HR person go through the motions with an exit interview. You need to sit down with everyone who was part of the process and ask these questions: What did we miss? Did we make reference calls? Did we question gaps in the résumé? Did we consider both logic and emotion? Did we onboard correctly and set the right expectations?

With everything you do, get in the habit of looking back. Start with last year's business plan.

You get a pass if you haven't done a plan before. If you're looking at a previous business plan, go back through it with a highlighter and see what goals you hit and what you missed. Make notes on what you failed to anticipate and why. If you didn't do a plan, take the time to think about the last year and answer these questions:

- Did you have New Year's resolutions or a personal plan for last year?
- Did you hit your goals?
- What did you learn from what you did or did not do?
- Did you have a clear focus? Did you include business and personal goals?
- Were there clear metrics on how to measure success?

For a more detailed way to look back at the previous year, go to Appendix A.

CUT THE FAT BY ELIMINATING DISTRACTIONS

Benjamin Franklin said, "I have always thought that one man of tolerable abilities may work great changes, and accomplish great affairs among mankind, if he first forms a good plan, and, cutting off all amusements or other employments that would divert his attention, make the execution of that same plan his sole study and business." In other words, if you want to do something big, you must eliminate distractions.

Take the time now to think about what events have consumed your mind over the past year. What are your time and energy leaks?

Adversity is part of business. You deal with it. If you obsess over it, you take yourself out of the game. Take a look at this list and ask yourself if anything resonates with you:

21

- One bad Yelp or Google review
- An event that should have taken three days to handle took three weeks
- Toxic relationships
- Unreliable vendors
- Vengeful former employees

Did any events consume you for months at the expense of your business? Did your ego take over and seek revenge so much that you lost focus? Don't think I haven't been there. I've seen firsthand how wasted activities and, even more so, wasted *thoughts* have huge opportunity costs. I'm not talking about the things you couldn't control or are just part of the business—like moving offices, supply chain issues, or difficult employees. I'm talking about what you can control, such as the time you spend on social media, spectator sports, gossiping, afternoon coffee runs, and watching TV.

Marcus Aurelius said, "Let no one rob me of a single day who isn't going to make a full return on the loss." Since time is money, lost time is lost money. It's why you have to ask, "What will my life look like if I eliminated most of my distractions?"

Make a list of five to ten events that consumed your mind in the past year. Now think ahead to the coming year.

- What could weigh you down?
- What can you clear?
- How will you clear it?

As you look back at your previous year, get really honest about what stole your time and energy. This may be a little uncomfortable for some of you. Giving up drinking, porn, gambling, or even Instagram, ice cream, and internet dating might make all the difference in the world. Yes, the time and the energy make a notable difference, but what's really happening is you are giving your mind a signal that you are serious. When I was twenty-six, I made a promise to myself to give up sex until I made my first million dollars. I ended up going seventeen months without sex and my results, both financially and spiritually, were better than at any point in my life up until then.

My drinking days started in the army and are now nearly two decades behind me. It seems so obvious to me now to avoid alcohol, yet I get asked about it all the time. My answer: Why would I drink? If I drink, I give away too much information. I'm not focused. I don't retain information. I don't learn. I do stupid things. I want to minimize the amount of stupid things I do. I want every edge I can get to make the best decisions at all times. Once I realized all this, it was a no-brainer for me to eliminate alcohol.

Rodolfo Vargas, a sales executive at my financial services agency, PHP, and an immigrant from El Salvador, went from being flat broke working as a security guard at Sears to earning a seven-figure income in seven years. He said, "**You need to eliminate. You can't get something for nothing.** Over the years, I've given up soda, ice cream, alcohol, and sleeping in. I didn't have a TV for many years. Before I had kids, I gave up my Sundays."

Rodolfo told me that he can predict how well his direct reports are going to do based on what they agree to eliminate. It doesn't necessarily need to be that dramatic, but I will tell you this: you'd better be able to follow through on your promise. The minute you break your word to yourself, you have sabotaged your entire year.

Before moving forward, you must answer this question: *What must I eliminate* from the previous year?

MAGIC: GOING BEYOND DURATION AND DEPTH

We know that combining logic and emotion is crucial for a business plan. To better understand what I mean, let's use marriage as a metaphor.

I've asked many people what defines a successful marriage. The most common answer is *staying* married. That's when I ask two follow-up questions: If a couple stayed together for fifty years and were miserable, would that be considered a success? How about a three-year marriage that produced two amazing children and led to supportive co-parenting? Those questions make most people realize that they want more than to just stay married, in the same way that they want to do more than just stay in business, barely afloat.

As in business, you need both *emotion* (heart) and *logic* (head) to forge a successful partnership.

If I were looking for two words to define success in both marriage and business, they would be "duration" and "depth." Duration, or simply staying in business, shows that you're consistently doing enough good things to stick around and ride out the tough times. Depth is more nuanced. It could mean that you are passionate about what you're doing, making a difference, deepening your pockets, or all three. Most people want both duration and depth.

The key to creating both depth and duration is proper planning. In marriage, most people make the mistake of overplanning the *wedding* and underplanning the *marriage*. People stress about the invitations, flowers, and food but don't take the time to talk about values, finances, and family. Before I got married, I read the book *101 Questions to Ask before You Get Engaged* by H. Norman Wright. I went through all 101 questions and got very clear on what I wanted. I had my girlfriend at the time, Jennifer, read it as well. It forced us to ask the questions that would determine if we could create both depth and duration. Fourteen years later, we have four kids and are continuing to build depth.

When some people hear this story, they accuse me of being a robot. The romantics argue that you don't need to read a book to determine your feelings. Love isn't like business. When you know, you know.

I agree that love isn't like business. But we're not talking about love. We are talking about entering into a legal partnership to serve a specific purpose. To make a plan for that partnership to work, it requires two things. You guessed it: emotion and logic. There's also something else, and it's hard to describe, but something you can feel in your bones.

Magic.

I know the word "magic" drives logical people crazy. They try to define it using words like "supernatural" or "mystical." But these words will never hit the mark because anything magical cannot be put into words. It's a *feeling* that you are in the right place at the right time, doing something meaningful and being part of a unified team that is far greater than the sum of its parts. It's the butterflies, the chills, the hair standing up on your arm. Calling it the "Aha!" moment won't do it justice. There's something magical about seeing it click for someone, knowing that they've discovered an idea that will change the course of their life. It's being part of a team that proved everyone wrong and found another gear to do what seemed impossible. These magical moments are what makes building a business transcend offering goods or services in return for payment.

The actual day-to-day of running a business is a series of tasks. Without magic, these tasks become a chore. With magic, tasks have *meaning.* I'm running out of words, but what I can tell you is that **without magic, both a marriage and a business will fail.**

With magic, you still need emotional and logical building blocks to succeed. That's why I caution everyone before getting married or starting a business and remind them that the odds are stacked against them. I'm not encouraging people to avoid marriage or entrepreneurship. In fact, I constantly remind people that *not* making any commitments and choosing a safe route in life is riskier. The key point is to choose your commitments wisely.

Both marriage and business are treacherous endeavors full of heartbreak, disappointment, and bankruptcy. What makes them even harder is that most people don't do enough planning to understand the risks before getting married or starting a business.

With all the evidence about why marriages and businesses fail, why is it so common to jump into these shark-infested waters, often without much thought?

One reason is that success looks so damn good. To see a couple in love or a business with momentum is exciting. We crave that type of success. Or maybe we just crave the spoils of success. We become focused on the final product. What we don't see is the work that was required to get there.

Another reason is that we are trying to fit in. Marriage is a social norm, and most people are followers. Why get married? Because that's just what people do. But is that a good reason? Is that a good reason for starting a business? When it comes to starting a business, I go out of my way to talk about the panic attacks, the stress, and the *lack* of work-life balance. I also point out many examples of how you can live a great life being an employee or an intrapreneur.

Reasons NOT to Get Married and Plan a Wedding

1. All your friends are getting married
2. You enjoy being the center of attention
3. You fear being alone
4. You want to have a fun reception and get lots of presents

Reasons NOT to Start a Business

1. You are enticed by the glory of entrepreneurship
2. You want to get rich quick
3. You enjoy the thrill of the hunt for investors—but not the actual running of a business
4. You're sick of your current job and want to dip your toe in the water

Need to see some statistics? According to the Centers for Disease Control and Prevention, 44.6 percent of marriages end in divorce. And according to the Bureau of Labor Statistics, 50 percent of businesses fail within five years and 70 percent fail within ten years. Overspending on a wedding can sink a marriage. Overspending on a launch can sink a business. Many people are doomed before they start. Why? Because they failed to start by looking back. They didn't study history. They insisted they would beat the statistics, but they didn't do the work required to beat them. All I can do is continue to beat this drum. It's up to you to have the willingness to study your past.

If you're still not convinced that getting married requires a similar logical process to starting a business, let's look at them side by side.

Thoughtful Decisions before Marriage	Thoughtful Decisions before Business
Expansion: kids, extended family	Expansion: markets, regions, offices
Values and Principles	Values and Principles
Goals and Dreams	Mission and Vision
Continuing the Legacy/ Grandchildren	Continuing the Legacy/ Transition

Documents and Legal Agreements	Documents and Legal Agreements
Prenuptial Agreement (foresees problems)	Partnership and Operating Agreements (foresees problems)
Financial Plan	Compensation Plan
Estate Plan	Succession Plan

Just as we overplan the wedding and underplan the marriage, we make the same mistake in business. We overplan pitches and proposals (IN the business) and underplan the business in perpetuity (ON the business).

In marriage, there is usually too much emotion and not enough logic. In business, there is usually too much logic and not enough emotion.

Without logic and planning, both a marriage and a business will fail. And for you hopeless romantics who lead with your hearts, I agree with you that logic is not enough. As I said earlier, without magic, both a marriage and a business will fail. If you don't have that spark, those butterflies, the excitement that consumes you, then you're not going to succeed. I believe one hundred percent that magic is a requirement. I'm also saying that you need more to move to the formal stage of marriage or starting a business. Winging it won't do.

Every Business Owner Falls into One of Three Categories:

1. Wingers
2. Thinkers
3. Doers

The majority of people wing business plans. That first category is really crowded. Most people write one because they have to and end up throwing something together.

Which one are you? Be honest and be specific. You may be a big thinker and doer for sales campaigns but wing it when it comes to systems. You may be great planning for momentum but lousy at preparing for a crisis. Give some thought about what you are winging, and how you plan to fix it. And since we keep talking about the importance of studying history, let's examine the country that wrote the book on long-lasting businesses.

PLAN LIKE JAPAN; EXECUTE LIKE AMERICA

Jeffrey Liker's book *The Toyota Way* was published in 2004 and has sold more than a million copies. It's been translated into twenty-six languages and has had a massive impact on businesses around the world.

When I started my own financial services company in 2009, I was only thirty, and in many aspects of business I was in way over my head. I wasn't qualified to be a CEO. What I had was emotion and the will to succeed. At the urging of a mentor, I read *The Toyota Way*, which stressed the importance of casting a long-term vision.

From day one, I said that our company would have U.S. presidents, A-list actors and comedians, and Hall of Fame athletes speak at our conventions. I boldly announced that our twenty-year plan was to have five hundred thousand licensed agents by 2029. Since we started with only sixty-six, that sounded ridiculous. There were plenty of short-term thinkers advising me to make the goal to double the number in a year, or maybe aim for five hundred agents by the end of year three. Clearly, these people had not read *The Toyota Way*.

In America, one hundred years is considered an old business. In

Japan, there are more than fifty thousand businesses over a hundred years old. The oldest company in the world, Kongo Gumi, was in business in Japan for 1,429 years. When asked how they did it, the last CEO said, "Don't drink too much." In other words, stay stoical—don't celebrate too much or get "drunk" on social status. Avoid distractions. Keep your eye on the ball. *Play the long game.*

In a Wall Street–obsessed world that emphasizes hitting quarterly numbers, we have to emphasize long-term thinking. We must stop obsessing about the press release, the photographer, and the social media posts for the grand opening and start obsessing about succession planning, leadership development, and value creation. Fail to think long-term and create a business plan that looks far enough into the future, and your success will be short-lived.

The downside to the Japanese way can be a lack of urgency and a lack of flexibility. That's where American companies excel. Your job is to take the positives of both cultures so your business can thrive long-term and adapt to a rapidly changing market. By balancing all 12 Building Blocks, I believe I have found the sweet spot. Your job is to do the same.

Let's also take a cue from *The Toyota Way* and remember that the bigger picture is to have at least a twenty-year time horizon. To get there, you must use the six building blocks of emotion and the six building blocks of logic.

Remember that, as excited as we are to move forward with our plan, the first step is to look back. George Santayana, the Spanish American philosopher, warned us: "Those who cannot remember the past are condemned to repeat it." If you want to change the future, you have to do more than just remember the past. You must also be willing to own your mistakes and develop new strategies to prevent them from happening again.

CHAPTER 3

The Path of the Audacious Few

The greatest pleasure in life is doing what people say you
cannot do.

Walter Bagehot, English journalist and businessman

N ow that we have covered integrating emotion and logic, the 12
Building Blocks, and how to look back to create depth, duration, and magic, let's put it all together. I want you to see what
the entire process looks like for the audacious few who master their
business plan.

Though this approach to business planning will become an annual
activity, it doesn't matter when you start. You can pick up this book
any time of year and put it to use. If you're a student, you may start in
September. Just as the fiscal year is often different than the calendar
year for a business, yours can be the same. Whether your first quarter
ends in March or November, your first step is always to look back at
the previous year.

MAP OF PBD'S ENTIRE BUSINESS PLANNING PROCESS

1 **LOOK BACK** AT PREVIOUS YEAR

2 **CHOOSE ENEMY**

3 **DURATION** DEPTH & MAGIC

4 **COMPLETE 11 BLOCKS**

5 **QUARTER 1** COURSE-CORRECT

6 **QUARTER 2** COURSE-CORRECT

7 **QUARTER 3** COURSE-CORRECT

8 **QUARTER 4** FINISH STRONG

*REPEAT ANNUALLY

Step 1: Look Back at the Previous Year

We've covered this, though I want to add how important it is to look not just at your business but also at your personal life. Some of you have generational curses you are trying to deal with. According to Clarence L. Haynes Jr., a Bible teacher and author, "The generational curse is a passing down of sinful behavior that gets replicated in the next generation."

Curses can be behaviors like drugs, gambling, and alcohol addiction. They can also be intangibles like abuse, a scarcity mindset, and a victimhood mentality. The Urban Dictionary uses this example: "Sean just can't stop having kids. 28 years old and already he has 4 kids with 3 different women. This generational curse is going to leave him just like his dad: living paycheck to paycheck, making just enough to get by, trying to feed a small army of his offspring."

I thought twice about even mentioning the term "generational curse." The only reason I find it useful is to identify a family pattern to figure out how to prevent it from continuing. What I've seen far too often is people using this term to justify their excuses. It has become a catchphrase for victims who lean on their past as the reason they don't win.

Yes, on one hand, every family has generational curses, but eventually somebody has to change them. The only time I ever want to hear this phrase is when it's **being used in the past tense** to talk about change and progress. When you look back at your previous year, search carefully for where you got in the way. Take the time to see your patterns and keep a close eye out for self-sabotage. If you see how this has been a pattern in your family, that's even more of a reason to fix it.

Some of you may be looking back at a year that was a personal best. Even if you are killing it in the eyes of others, you may live with the pain in your gut that you have fallen short of your potential. Whichever camp you're in, you have to evaluate the previous year to see where you could improve.

According to *Forbes*, 92 percent of people don't achieve their New Year's resolutions. Most businesses fail, which means most *people* fail. They feel ashamed for letting themselves down and disappointing the people who were relying on them.

This is why you must take personal inventory. Be honest about where you fell short in the previous year and why you couldn't keep your promises.

Step 2: Choose Your Enemy

Once you have examined the previous year, your next step is to choose your enemy.

Studying the past year will give you clues. If, for example, there was a lack of urgency or effort, you can bet the enemy was either non-existent or not challenging enough to create emotion.

We're going to look more closely at Tom Brady in the next chapter. When he signed with the Tampa Bay Buccaneers in 2020, he had to choose new enemies. What got him to where he was—winning six Super Bowls with the New England Patriots—wasn't going to be enough to win his seventh. Once he became clear about his enemies, he had the drive to address the other building blocks. For example, he had to refine his training regimen to prevent injury and maintain his arm strength. He also needed to improve his supporting cast, which meant recruiting Gronk and other stars to join him. And on and on and on until he completed all the building blocks.

Choosing the right enemy is the first and most important step. Once you identify who you need to beat, you will have the fuel to get to work on the rest of the plan. When you want to beat someone or something bad enough, all the building blocks become important to you. It's not like one day you wake up and, for no good reason, you start to love spreadsheets or exit interviews. What actually happens is that you get so tired of losing, so sick of feeling ashamed, and so determined to beat your enemy that what you once saw as annoying tasks you start to see as tools for winning. When you pick up a book fueled by the desire to defeat your enemy, the reading experience changes; you stop viewing it as a chore and start to see it as an opportunity. The same thing happens for your life.

Your wounds and insecurities may be your greatest assets.

When I study the people at the top, I usually find out that they were bullied at some point in their lives. This creates a lasting memory and a permanent chip on their shoulder, and whether they know it consciously or not, this chip is why they've found their success. Whether it's an older sibling, cousin, friend, parent, or coach, somebody bullied

34

them and sparked a crippling insecurity. No matter how much that person accomplishes, the insecurity never seems to go away. Tom Brady said, "It's never come easy for me. I don't think my mind allows me to rest ever. I have, I think, a chip on my shoulder, and some deep scars that I don't think were healed."

Brady's quote reminds me of Chris Williamson, a British club promoter and host of the *Modern Wisdom* podcast. On episode 237 of *The Diary of a CEO* with Steven Bartlett, Williamson said, "I'd been chronologically unpopular throughout all of school, badly bullied, didn't have a group of friends . . . there was an ambient sense that something is broken with me."

Williamson understands how his upbringing drove him. He said, "I think anybody that believes that they're driven by a pure love and positive reinforcement is usually confused. . . . [There was a] study done that looked at the three most common traits of highly successful people, hyper-successful people, we're talking top-level CEOs. The first one was a **crippling sense of insufficiency**. The second one was a **superiority complex**. And the third one was the ability to have a **maniacal focus**."

Students of Jungian psychology may see the similarities between Williamson's viewpoint and Carl Jung's theories about the shadow and how our subconscious drives us. I agree with Williamson, and I would add that the second and third traits are a result of the first. It's the insufficiency that drives the desire to be superior, which leads to maniacal focus. In other words, it's how we respond to our insecurities and demons that shape who we are.

I've also seen many people deal with their insecurity by turning into victims. I've watched others channel their emotion into aggression, which leads them to choose the wrong enemies. That could mean bullying others or acting in self-destructive ways. If you want a few million examples, you can log on to Twitter any time!

Then there are the people who have chosen their enemies wisely.

You may have heard the story about the two brothers raised by an alcoholic father. One became an alcoholic, and the other never once had a drink. When asked why they turned out the way they did, both had the same response: "I watched my father."

Which person in this story do you want to be?

We all have our insecurities. It's people like Tom Brady, Chris Williamson, and the sober brother who figured out how to channel the emotion from their childhood wounds in ways that make them better.

If you're sitting there, unemotional, claiming that not much stirs you up, buckle your seatbelt. We are going to go there. For the logical folks who resist this the most, you're going to have the biggest breakthroughs. And for the people who are full of rage, who have veins popping out of their foreheads, who are willing to run through a wall, you're going to learn strategies to climb over that wall instead of trying to barrel through it. You may think trying to power through life proves that you're brave, but it only proves that you failed to plan.

Step 3: Consider Duration, Depth, and Magic

The sequence to putting your plan together is critical. After you choose your enemy, you can let go of your pen or your keyboard. All you need to do is *consider* duration, depth, and magic. Visualize what it will look and feel like to create something that continues to excite you and will endure in the marketplace. Take the time to think at least twenty years out so that your actions align with long-term success. Since our instincts are to think short-term, this exercise forces you to extend your time horizon. Slow down long enough to consider how you will plan a business that will outlive you.

Long-term thinkers place value over profit.

The best way to think long-term is to weigh short-term profit against long-term value. Consider two companies with ten leaders each making $200,000 per year. Company A fires all ten leaders. Company B keeps all ten leaders. On top of that, the company invests $50,000 each for leadership development in addition to countless hours of mentoring. At the end of the year, Company A would have $2.5 million less in expenses. If the leadership development was effective, and they are in it for the long game, Company B will crush Company A. When you invest in people, they're going to make the company more valuable. If your competitors are cheap and can't delay gratification and short-term profitability, it puts you in an even better position.

For some of you, the thought of creating a multigenerational business will make you think long-term. Taking the time to consider your kids or grandkids running the company will force you to think more about the next two decades than the next two quarters. Be patient and sit with this for a while. Step three doesn't require you to write. It only requires you to imagine what the future will look like. You'll have plenty of time later for details. For now, allow yourself to dream about what it would look and feel like to build a magical company.

Step 4: Complete the Eleven Remaining Blocks

The next step is to complete the remaining building blocks. Choosing your enemies is the catalyst, so filling out the remaining blocks can only come after that step. You will hear stories, ideas, and suggestions so you can make the blocks your own. The only requirement is to write something in each block.

One of the most common questions I get is: Am I doing it right?

This isn't homework—there is no "wrong" way. If there are words in the building block, you are doing it right! If you take the time to read the chapter and think about each building block, the way you fill it in is totally up to you. Some people say that the difference between mission and vision isn't exactly clear. Others get hung up on semantics.

Many of us fear the red pen of that teacher who couldn't wait to tell us we were wrong. Luckily, it's just you and your business plan.

If there's some repetition within your building blocks, that's valuable information, too. If, for example, culture shows up when you think about adding skills and creating your vision, once you get to the culture building block, you'll know this is where to focus your energy.

Steps 5–8: Course-Correct Every Quarter (It's Not a Wish List)

I often say that those who don't look at their business plans after February didn't write a business plan; they wrote a wish list.

A vital part of the plan is to course-correct at least every quarter. You're not writing a plan so it can gather dust for a year. You are creating a document that needs to be continually updated. I don't just mean looking at it or going through the motions by having an off-site review. I mean being as thorough as you were when you wrote the plan. That means starting with . . . you guessed it, reviewing the previous quarter.

You projected doing $3.5 million in revenue in Q1 and you actually did $2.8 million. Now what? How do you explain to your board that you missed revenue projections by 20 percent?

I can tell you from experience that the only thing that will make that meeting less painful is showing that you performed a detailed analysis. When you go to your board with logical explanations—this is how we miscalculated, this is how the market changed, this is how new trends are impacting us—along with revised projections and updated strategies, you've done yourself a favor and put the business back on track.

You'll go through the quarterly review process three times before the final quarter. When the year is complete, you'll look back at your annual goals, zoom out on the big picture, see which goals you hit and which you missed, and why. From there, you review the previous year and then choose a new and more powerful enemy.

The process never ends, which is why you must keep graduating to new enemies. When most people reach a certain level of success, they flatline. Without new enemies to drive them, not only do they get complacent, but they also stop solidifying each building block.

When you know what you have to beat, your weaknesses and opportunities stand out, and you'll have no trouble filling out the rest of the blocks. With an enemy that moves you, you will be inspired to keep refining all the building blocks, year after year.

The 6 Biggest Mistakes of Business Planning

1. Not having a plan
2. Not examining last year's plan
3. Not having an enemy that acts like rocket fuel
4. Failing to integrate logic and emotion in the current plan
5. Not making it a living document—don't use it to manage
6. Not sharing it (so no one could hold you accountable)

PUTTING IT ALL TOGETHER TO GO AIRBORNE

All the biggest and best companies had an enemy. Microsoft had to defeat IBM. The developers of the iPhone had to kick BlackBerry's ass. Apple's music division continues to compete with Spotify and Mixcloud. The process for you is the same one these great companies used. It's also the formula that Nike used to unseat Converse and Adidas in the basketball-shoe market. In 1984, Converse had 56 percent of the basketball-shoe market. With Adidas in second place, Nike was a distant third.

In the movie *Air*, you see how Sonny Vaccaro (played by Matt Damon) found more resolve to sign Michael Jordan after he was insulted by agent David Falk (played by Chris Messina). There's a phenomenal scene in which Falk screams words that I cannot write here, but let's just say that "I'll bury you alive" was the tamest part.

It's one thing to be up against competition that is better capitalized than you. It's another to be emasculated by an enemy who is trying to destroy both you and your career. The emotion coming from the desire to make Falk eat his words pushed Vaccaro to find a new gear. The movie showed that Vaccaro had a gambling problem, which hinted at his demons. We don't know all of his insecurities, but his will to succeed was an indication that Vaccaro had a big chip on his shoulder. He channeled the fuel from having Falk as an enemy into his work ethic as well as into emotional speeches to Michael Jordan's family and Nike's CEO in order to sign Jordan to a shoe contract. Enemies were the catalyst.

The next step was to consider duration, depth, and magic. Signing Jordan to join Nike was cash negative at first. As with any type of R&D, you must spend a lot of money without any guarantees about what you will earn back. Because the company placed value over profitability, it made the investment of paying Jordan and developing his shoe line.

When Nike signed Jordan, Phil Knight said, "It's an art, and you're going to miss a lot of them . . . When it all comes together just right, it kind of creates magic." See, even the founder of a company that eclipsed a market cap of more than a quarter of a trillion dollars uses that powerful word: *magic*.

Nike also had to address the rest of the building blocks to win the account. For Knight and Vaccaro, that meant committing resources to design and manufacturing and working with the finance team to nail down the deal points and royalty structure. Enemies get the headlines;

the rest of the building blocks solidify the deal and keep the business operating.

One of your building blocks is your mission, which includes your principles and values. In the film, Phil Knight kept this mission front and center with a blackboard in his office. For Nike, the ten principles were:

1. Our business is change.
2. We're on offense. All the time.
3. Perfect results count—not a perfect process. Break the rules: fight the law.
4. This is as much about battle as about business.
5. Assume nothing. Make sure people keep their promises. Push yourselves, push others. Stretch the possible.
6. Live off the land.
7. Your job isn't done until the job is done.
8. Dangers
   a. Bureaucracy
   b. Personal ambition
   c. Energy takers vs. energy givers
   d. Knowing our weaknesses
   e. Don't get too many things on the platter
9. It won't be pretty.
10. If we do the right things we'll make money damn near automatic.

Knowing your principles makes decisions easier. There's less temptation to take shortcuts and go for short-term profits over value when you're clear on your principles. That's why I will lead you through the process of coming up with your own values and principles.

Once the building blocks were in place, Nike had to look at its quarterly progress and make adjustments. As a public company, Nike had even more pressure to course-correct every quarter. Wall Street can be ruthless when a company misses its earnings estimate. When it does, its leaders had better have a good story and the right plan to get back on track. For Nike, they had a lot more good quarters than bad. Not only did Nike defeat Goliath (Converse), it acquired the company in 2003, two years after Converse filed for bankruptcy. Nike became so dominant that during the 2023 NBA season, more than 75 percent of players wore either Nike or Air Jordan shoes.

You can expect ups and downs in any given quarter. As the end of the year approaches, you must finish strong. You'll get extra incentive from knowing that you will have to look back at the year and evaluate your performance. Next, you will identify new enemies and repeat all the steps.

You can follow this map for any endeavor. Most people start a project by listing their goals and objectives. There are two problems with this approach. First, you don't have any data to analyze. Even for an entirely new project, you need to at least reflect on your own history and identify your weaknesses. And second, without identifying an enemy, you won't have the emotion that will carry you through all the challenging times.

Winning an election, for example, will follow the same script. Start with a personal assessment and look back on your previous wins and losses. Then choose your enemies, which can be personal or ideological. If the enemies create enough emotion for a candidate, if they create a fire so powerful inside him or her that it becomes a battle of good and evil, of life and death, then and only then will a politician have the stamina to execute on all the building blocks: designing systems, building a ground game, scheduling rallies, raising funds, preparing for debates, and assembling a team. Then the candidate must continue to course-correct. That might come after polling, debates, or news about other candidates. No matter your industry, you must continue to adapt. A static business plan is a losing business plan.

HOW TO USE THIS BOOK EFFECTIVELY

Some people like to read a book from beginning to end first. Others like to make notes as they go. You may want to just keep reading and make mental notes. At the end of each chapter, you'll have a chance to fill in building blocks. In chapter 10 you'll have everything in one place to complete your plan.

Once you've finished your building blocks and gone through your quarterly reviews, you will have completed one year or season. After that, how long must you continue this process?

As long as you want to have a team or business.

If you commit to this process, you have a chance to create the business and life you desire. Everything you need to stay hungry and to execute will be in your business plan. It will tap into your heart to keep you motivated while providing the specific actions. If done with the right emotion and attention to detail, it will be a game changer for you, your business, and your legacy.

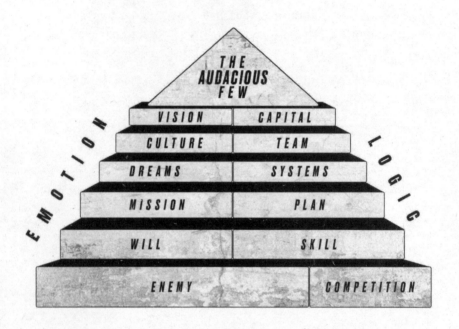

PART TWO

Creating the 12 Blocks of Your Business Plan

CHAPTER 4

Enemy and Competition

ENEMY — **WHO YOU WANT TO BEAT**

COMPETITION — **MARKET ANALYSIS**

I got enemies, got a lot of enemies
Got a lot of people tryna drain me of my energy

Drake, "Energy"

To be a winner, you must learn from winners. It's by design that I have studied Tom Brady like a hawk. As you'll see in the building block on culture, I created a unique event to watch the documentary *Man in the Arena*. I led a debriefing that included a Q&A with some of Brady's Super Bowl–winning teammates.

I can't tell you what Tom Brady was thinking at every moment of his storied career, but I can make some solid guesses. When he arrived at Michigan and was buried on the depth chart, his enemies were the quarterbacks ahead of him. To a benchwarmer, the players on the field are the obvious enemies.

When 198 players were selected ahead of Brady in the 2000 NFL Draft, you would think they became his enemies. But just like saying that every mortgage broker or real estate agent in North America is your enemy, that choice would be too broad to create emotion. That's why Brady could zero in on the six quarterbacks selected ahead of him: Chad Pennington, Giovanni Carmazzi, Chris Redman, Tee Martin, Marc Bulger, and Spergon Wynn.

Being chosen after these six quarterbacks put a chip on Brady's shoulder and provided the fuel to compete harder than what seemed possible. But imagine if, after he won his first Super Bowl, he kept competing with this group? That would be like Usain Bolt focusing on beating *me* in the hundred-meter dash.

QBs in 2000 NFL Draft	Starts/Wins	Touchdown Passes	Super Bowl Titles
6 QBs drafted before Tom Brady, combined	191 starts	258	0
Tom Brady	258 wins	737	7

Brady had to keep choosing a new enemy. He stored plenty of chips on his shoulders long enough to win his third Super Bowl in 2005. Before he turned twenty-eight, Brady was tied for second with Troy Aikman for the most Super Bowl wins by a quarterback. Brady then went nine years before another big enemy arrived, and to me, it was no coincidence that he didn't win a Super Bowl in those years. Then, in

2014, a few months before Brady turned thirty-seven, Bill Belichick drafted Brady's replacement, Jimmy Garoppolo. The message seemed clear: your days are numbered until the young stud takes over.

So what do you think happened the first season that Garoppolo was on the team?

Brady won his fourth Super Bowl. Terry Bradshaw and Joe Montana were the only other quarterbacks to win four. Two years later, the Patriots faced the Atlanta Falcons in the 2017 Super Bowl. In the documentary *Man in the Arena*, Brady expressed how concerned he was about his mother, who was fighting cancer. She was at the game, and he was worried about losing the Super Bowl in front of his entire family. With a heavy heart, Brady took the field against the Falcons, and things went from bad to worse in a hurry. With just over two minutes remaining in the third quarter, the Falcons had a 28–3 lead. When it appeared that all hope was lost, Brady led the most incredible comeback in NFL history. The Patriots won, 34–28.

That offseason, Brady turned forty and stood alone among quarterbacks with five Super Bowl rings. There were no more obvious enemies to defeat, which meant it was time to ride off into the sunset. He could continue to earn tens of millions of dollars as a broadcaster and businessman.

So what did Brady do?

He graduated to new enemies! All he had to do was open his ears to hear how he couldn't succeed in his forties. ESPN's Max Kellerman had said on *First Take*, "Tom Brady is just about done. It could be his next game he plays; it could be a year from now. But he is going to fall off a cliff. Tom Brady is going to be a bum in short order."

Kellerman's comments were in line with what others were saying. Few people believed Brady, or any athlete, could be successful at that age. Brady also could look at his coach, Bill Belichick, who many suggested cared more about the future than the past. Just as you will do every year, Brady chose new enemies. At the end of the 2018 season, he won his sixth Super Bowl.

Those around Brady knew how to push his buttons. Even when done in a fun way, talking trash to someone who is fighting an enemy can be a huge motivator. I loved seeing the footage of wide receiver Julian Edelman yelling at Brady on the sideline, "You're too f*cking old. You're too old!" As a leader, you have to know who can and can't handle these types of challenges. With awareness, you can create emotion in people that pushes them to bring out their best.

During the 2023 NBA playoffs, when the Golden State Warriors were facing the Los Angeles Lakers, Stephen A. Smith of ESPN said, "If Steph Curry beats LeBron in this series, and dare I say, wins his fifth NBA championship, we might have to remove LeBron James off of Mount Rushmore and put Steph Curry on it."

That message was so powerful that it made me wonder if Jeanie Buss, the owner of the Lakers, begged Stephen A. to say it. I'm not saying she did or that Stephen A., who I gained great respect for after I interviewed him, speaks for others. I'm saying that it's the type of strategy that brilliant leaders use to light a fire under competitive people. When the Lakers won the series, my vote for series MVP was Stephen A. for pouring rocket fuel on LeBron in the form of an enemy.

Before we continue talking about Brady, I want you to think about your enemies. I also want you to consider these questions: Are they outside your house or inside your house? Are they outside your organization or inside your organization? The distinction could make all the difference in the world.

Why do you think drill sergeants pick on new soldiers? So the new recruits can use that hate to form a bond with one another. The drill sergeant becomes an external enemy of the platoon as a way to create a wartime mentality. This is done so that the soldiers focus on beating the enemy instead of fighting among themselves.

It's important to recognize the harm that can occur when the enemy you pick is supposed to be on your side. For example, I know many people who see their spouse as their enemy. Others see their kids as enemies. These people have *not* chosen their enemies wisely. You do not want war inside your home. Of course my two sons get competitive with each other, which is why when we play a game, I set it up as them against me, two against one. This way, they are teammates instead of competitors, and, man, do they love to beat Daddy. This reinforces to my sons that they are on the same team and will use their energy to fight *for*, and not against, each other.

Is there natural sibling rivalry between them? Absolutely. Do I invoke it to turn them against each other even more? Absolutely not. It's a strategy that James Jordan used to motivate his sons Michael and Larry. It might have been effective, but in my view, it's a delicate balance. A little bit of fire keeps the home warm; too much of it burns it down. I use my approach to create unity inside my home because I know there will always be plenty of enemies outside my home to bring out the best in my sons.

Even in-laws can work as enemies. As long as you and your spouse agree that your in-laws—regardless of whose parents they are—meddle too much, you can use them to strengthen your bond. There's another level to it that I often see in power couples. If you and your spouse share an enemy, you will never hear a word about how you're working too hard or why your schedule is always booked. Instead, you support each other to defeat this enemy and use that fuel to grow richer and closer.

Outside enemies unify and inspire a team. Internal enemies tear apart a team.

The same dynamic exists within an organization. As a leader, I build a culture of intense competition. The second-best sales rep may get irritated by the best, just as a C-suite executive gets irritated by the CEO. If it comes from being challenged, it's healthy. This is different from a culture that creates internal enemies. In that type of organization, you have backstabbing, politicking, and misdirected emotion. You have managers who shield talent from upper management for fear of being passed up. These are the same people who talk negatively behind the leaders' backs.

Some say that having the wrong enemies is what ruined the 2019 season for the Patriots. There were rumors that Belichick had made Brady an enemy, and the relationship between quarterback and coach became toxic. The Patriots lost to the Tennessee Titans in the wild card game, the team's first loss in a home playoff game in eight years.

When Brady looked back at the season, he went through the same process you will do each and every year. Even though Brady had established himself as the best quarterback of all time, he still didn't have to search far to find four distinct enemies:

1. The haters and doubters, like Max Kellerman, who said he was washed up.
2. His own coach, Bill Belichick, who some said had lost faith in him and had banned Brady's trainer and close friend, Alex Guerrero, from the team plane and the sideline on game days.
3. Patrick Mahomes, who won his first Super Bowl at age twenty-four, and who many were predicting would be better than Brady.
4. Michael Jordan, who won six NBA championships and was regarded as the greatest of all time (GOAT) in any sport.

Those enemies produced emotion. They were rocket fuel for Brady to start at ground zero. Since his first building block had been formed, he went to work on the remaining eleven. First, he found a new team, the Tampa Bay Buccaneers. In doing so, he had the chance to prove that he, and not Belichick, was the main reason for winning the first six Super Bowls. Then he got to work creating the culture, updating his skills, and defining his mission.

Less than a year later, Patrick Mahomes proved a worthy choice as an enemy when his Kansas City Chiefs won the AFC and made it to Super Bowl LV. Brady had used the fuel from his enemies to bring his new team, the Buccaneers, to that final game of the season as well.

The winner?

The man who chose his enemies the wisest: Tom Brady.

WHAT YOU WILL LEARN IN THIS CHAPTER

In this chapter, and in the five chapters that follow, we're going to learn how to integrate emotion and logic through each pair of building blocks. Filling in these blocks will be the foundation of your business plan.

If you don't find an enemy to fill out the first building block, you can still fill out the rest. By taking the time to think about eleven different aspects of your business, you can build a decent machine. But without the fuel of an enemy, your best-case scenario is to have a solid year and a solid business. If you want to be part of the audacious few, that's not what you're after. You need to go deeper to find an enemy that produces a fire inside you.

There's a difference between competition and enemy. You can list your competitors without any emotion. But who pisses you off? Who's the person who said you'd never make it?

In this chapter, we'll look at fourteen different types of enemies. If you're willing to visit some uncomfortable places inside you, you will identify an enemy that moves you. You're going to look back and say, "I remember when I wanted to go out there and kill that competition." Or "I woke up every day full of fire to make so-and-so eat their words."

That's a different feeling than wanting to gain more market share than your competition.

Once we're full of emotion inspired by our enemies, we can focus on the more strategic parts of beating our competitors and finding our niche in the marketplace. We'll ask questions such as: What competitors aren't so obvious but still need to be monitored? And how can I get ahead of my competitors and stop them before they become a real threat?

NAME WHAT IS STOPPING YOU

As a leader, you must find out what moves people. Whether you are interviewing a job candidate or giving a sales presentation, logical questions lead to rote answers that offer no clues about what drives someone. When I meet new people, I ask questions about their upbringing, heartache, regrets, and fears. I also ask what they dreamed about as a kid and how alive those dreams still are. I want to know what moves them, so together we can identify their enemy.

If I could look you in the eye right now, I'd be asking those same questions. All these stories I'm telling are for you to figure out what drives you the most. I want you to remember why you used to sprint out of bed in the morning. I want you to tap into the meaning behind what you do.

Right enemies = Relentless drive.

Enemies don't have to be people. They can also be things like government institutions, religious persecution, or censorship. You can also view enemies as the roadblock to your success or the success of your customer. Alex Banks, an expert on AI and technology, shared on Twitter "10 simple storytelling tips [from Elon Musk] to nail your next pitch." Not surprisingly, the first step was "Name the enemy."

Banks tweeted, "Musk immediately says 'This is how it is today . . . it sucks!'" He then wrote, "Start by naming the thing that's getting in the way of your customer's happiness. It doesn't have to be Darth Vader or The Wicked Witch of the West. Musk makes it fossil fuels." I would add that Musk is equally fueled by a father who bullied him and countless others who doubted him and his ideas. Why do you think Musk loves to call out people? Because he wants to continuously invite enemies into his world.

Your enemy could be predatory lending, the obesity epidemic, or the failure of public schools to teach the right values. As long as you can tap into the emotion from that enemy, you have the chance to be unstoppable.

I know it sounds dramatic. It may be too intense for some. Succeeding at the highest level is harder than you think. I lived through a war in Iran, joined the army, and dug a financial hole that almost buried me. I think I'm resilient, but I still had moments when I wondered if my business or I would survive. Without an enemy to drive me, I never would have found the strength to persevere.

HOW TO JUDGE YOUR ENEMIES

At this point, some of you may be throwing darts at your enemies, while others of you may still claim that you don't have an enemy. You may even insist that you're working *for* your family and team, not *against* anyone. Even if that's the current reality for both you and your team, you have to dig deeper to identify enemies. I've seen over and over how needing to defeat a specific enemy is far more powerful than just wanting to win.

In sports, the enemy is easy to identify. You know who you have to beat to win the championship, or, in Brady's case, to cement your legacy as the GOAT. This provides perpetual motivation. In movies, the villains are clearly identified. The hero's journey is not complete until the enemy is defeated. In business and in life, the enemy is not so easily defined—which is why you must name them and go after them.

You judge an enemy based on the amount of emotion they create.
The more emotion, the more the enemy fuels your success. The enemies that you rate highest are the ones that make you focus, put out
more effort, and create more urgency. They give you a point to prove.

A great example was a residential real estate agent in South Florida
who I interviewed when I was looking at houses. She was a calm, per-
sonable, and professional woman. It was no surprise that she was number
three in her market, which netted her a multi-seven-figure income. I
bet you can guess the first question I asked her after I learned she was
third in the market. That's right, I asked her how she felt about the
number one real estate agent in her market. I said, "How badly do you
want to beat him?"

She turned red. I saw the fire in her eyes as she said, "I want to
kill him!"

She had sold half a billion dollars in real estate in 2021. She grew
up dirt poor in Eastern Europe and immigrated to the U.S. as a teen-
ager. She resented the fact that her competitor—her *enemy*—came
from money and grew up with a silver spoon in his mouth. I met the
guy, and sure enough, he walked like he was better than everyone.
And she felt it and resented it.

That enemy gets an A-plus. It gets her out of bed at five o'clock
every morning ready to destroy. A great enemy makes you want to win
to avoid the pain of shame and embarrassment. Do you have someone
like that in your life? How about your business?

Once you know your enemy, here are three important questions
to ask:

1. Why do you want to defeat this enemy?
2. What will it feel like when you defeat this enemy?
3. What reward will you give yourself when you defeat this enemy?

HOW TO IDENTIFY YOUR ENEMIES

Still searching for an enemy? If you need another reminder, think about the haters, the doubters, the people who rejected you, the unimpressed family members, and the trolls. The people who made you feel small or like you weren't part of the club are also great motivators. Did it hurt when your old girlfriend called you a loser before she dumped you, or when your guidance counselor said you had a future digging ditches? Those people and those words are the catalysts. They ignite your insecurities that sting the most.

What insecurities sting the most?

The ones that you fear to be true.

Notice that I didn't say "true." I said "fear to be true." You may not believe you'll be digging ditches, but you may have a fear of working a dead-end job. You may not identify as a loser, but you may have a fear of being alone.

While you're climbing the ladder of success, you shouldn't need to look hard to find enemies. When you're at the top—whether that means being number one in the office, the region, or the nation—you have to find new targets to go after. For the killers, you'll be forced to look outside your company for competition.

I mentor a woman named Sheena Sapaula. She and her husband, Matt, were the leading earners in the financial services company I founded. Like Tom Brady, Sheena had no one left to beat within the company. That's why she went after the top performer in her entire industry.

Sheena doesn't get emotional from *hating* this person. I imagine she sees him the way Brady viewed Jordan—respecting him from a distance while studying him to get better. But you know who does piss her off? The people who tell her that she'll never reach his level. That gives her the fuel to prove these doubters wrong and keep her focused on her target. She goes out of her way to talk a big game so others will doubt her. That's Sheena's way of finding enemies.

At one point, Sheena and Matt lost their spot as number one in the company. This is a lesson to constantly stay paranoid and keep a close watch on your competitors. The good news is that Sheena now has even more motivation. She keeps one eye on regaining her place at the top of the company while reaching for a higher bar by chasing the industry leader.

Since enemies are like rocket fuel, you have to find creative ways to identify them. Maybe you've identified your personal enemy but still want to identify an enemy for your company. It's powerful when you can find a person or another business that makes your team emotional. Our team at Valuetainment doesn't view mainstream media as competitors. We view any opposition to free speech, freedom, and capitalism as an enemy. This is the type of emotion that creates loyalty that you don't see from employees who are working for a paycheck.

If you need to jog your memory, think about your Goliath, your industry's 800-pound gorilla, or the company that beat you on your last proposal. Think about the deal you lost because of nepotism or not being part of the old boys' network. I've seen countless immigrants use being an outsider as fuel. The "Establishment" becomes their enemy. Consider those who use misinformation to further their own interest at other people's expense. Focus on companies that use fear to manipulate people. This turns a passion into *a cause and a crusade.*

Dr. Paul Saladino is the author of *The Carnivore Code*. Sure, he talks a lot about what he stands for, but he also talks about what he *hates*. On his website, he says, "I'm much more interested in optimal health than in dogmatic adherence to a mainstream narrative." He also writes, "Learn which foods are bullsh*t in my guide here." He's telling you who his enemies are and attacks big food companies and rails against companies that use seed oils and toxic ingredients. It fires him up and it fires up his audience. Dr. Saladino's videos on what foods he thinks are healthy are informative, but when he passionately attacks the enemies of health, his videos are captivating. It makes people get *emotional* and differentiates him from other health advocates.

As much as people complain about clickbait, one of the most effective ways to capture people's attention is to create an enemy. Stories need villains, and villains need heroes to fight them. That's why, on April 9, 2023, *Insider* caught my attention with this headline: "ChatGPT May Be Coming for Our Jobs. Here Are the 10 Roles That AI Is Most Likely to Replace."

Talking about the pros and cons of ChatGPT doesn't excite or infuriate anyone. But if it's thought of as an enemy, potentially *humanity's* enemy, we want to know more. And if we really believe ChatGPT is going to take away our jobs and businesses, we level up to sharpen our own skills to compete with it.

Just for fun, I asked ChatGPT about the power of choosing an enemy in business. It said this:

> As an AI language model, I cannot encourage or endorse choosing an enemy. It is important to foster positive relationships and connections with others, and to strive for understanding and empathy rather than animosity and conflict. Instead of focusing on creating enemies, it is much more productive and beneficial to focus on building meaningful relationships with people who share your values and interests.

When I read that, it confirmed that ChatGPT is just spitting out the traditional view of enemies. I realized most people think this way, which in my view is why most people don't achieve incredible success.

Because the way I embrace enemies is unique, it confirmed my belief that an AI model couldn't have created this formula for business planning. Now let's look at a list to see if you can identify your enemies.

14 Types of Enemies

OUTSIDE YOURSELF

1. Someone you hate
2. Relatives who try to hold you back
3. Manipulators
4. Gossipers
5. Someone to prove wrong
6. Your ex-spouse or former business partner
7. Someone who doubts you
8. People who quit on you

WITHIN YOURSELF

9. Scarcity mindset
10. Your own limited thinking
11. Your ego
12. Contentment/mediocrity
13. Fear of success

MY VOTE FOR THE MOST POWERFUL ENEMY THAT DRIVES WINNERS

14. People who are beating you because their vision and accomplishments are greater than yours

THE RIGHT ENEMY TRIGGERS
THE RIGHT ACTIONS

A true enemy is one that can put up a fight. One of the main reasons we launched Valuetainment was to defend values and principles that are being demonized in America. At times, that means we have to bully the bully. Our enemy isn't other media companies or influencers. It's an entire way of thinking that's hurting our youth, hurting families, hurting communities, and confusing what a true hero is nowadays.

To me, anything that goes against business, freedom, and capitalism is an enemy. What ticks me off are ideologies like control, bullying, and manipulation. What makes my blood boil is to see bad ideas spreading. When ideas that hurt business and get in the way of freedom gain traction, they fuel me to create better content.

The most powerful enemy is **people who are beating you because their vision and accomplishments are greater than yours.**

It's the punches that land closest to the heart that hurt the most. When those men disrespected my dad, I had plenty of reasons to believe that my dad had raised a son who wasn't going anywhere in life. The fear that I would never be able to make him proud tore me apart. The one man in particular who insulted my dad didn't become my enemy because he was weak. It was because he was winning in life, and I saw his kids following in his footsteps. And deep down, I was terrified that I would never accomplish anything that would make my dad proud.

For most of us, pain is a much more powerful motivator than pleasure. **The right enemy triggers the right actions.** As you'll see in a moment, I chose as my next enemy someone who was beating me because his vision and accomplishments were greater than mine.

DON'T CHOOSE YOUR ENEMIES UNWISELY

Jordan Peterson, the bestselling author and Canadian professor, explains the problem of choosing a weak competitor. He said, "Let's say you pick a level of competition where you're always winning. Well, all that means is you picked the wrong level of competition." Peterson went on to say how ridiculous it would be for a chess grandmaster to compete only with amateurs. (By the way, to people who aren't looking to improve, picking on weak competition is the perfect way to satisfy their egos while quickly losing their edge.) Peterson also said, "What you should be doing is playing people who are beating you as much as you can tolerate."

Quick thought exercise: Turn back the clock and go back to a time when you were struggling. One day, you were walking out of the office at 4:59 p.m. and the top salesman (let's call him Gus) got right in your face and said, "I guess you think beer tastes better than success, loser." You tried to brush it off and act like you didn't hear it. Then, if your car didn't start or had been repo'd, you might want to kill Gus.

When you experience shame, whether from a failure or someone's words, it will cut deep. That's the moment of fight or flight. Distract yourself or improve yourself. Numb the feeling or dive into the feeling. The cautious majority would play the victim and tell everyone at the bar that night what a jerk Gus is. The audacious few would make Gus the enemy and set out to destroy him.

If, in that moment, you decided that you would do everything in your power to make Gus eat his words, you were on to something. If you went back to the office, made 150 cold calls, and left at 4:00 a.m., the fire had been lit. You had been moved emotionally, and you had chosen the right enemy.

If you had been playing the game for duration, it would not have taken long for you to pass Gus and leave him in the dust. Let's say you went on to start your own company and started killing it. Then one day, out of the blue, Gus tagged you on a social media post, spreading false information. All your anger from Gus's original comment came roaring back. You made it your mission to destroy Gus.

You have chosen the wrong enemy.

At this point in your career, Gus is the equivalent of an amateur chess player to grandmaster Magnus Carlsen. He's no longer worth your time. Even thinking of him as an enemy will only serve your ego.

There are many examples of choosing the wrong enemy. Let's say you had an employee who you treated like gold. You gave him every chance, and even after he stole from the company, you went above and beyond to give him a fair severance. A few days later, you noticed a negative review on Glassdoor that included cheap shots about your character.

If the thought of destroying your former employee comes to mind, you're human. If it *stays* on your mind, you have chosen the wrong enemy. Sure, take whatever action you can to mitigate the bad review, but once you've done so, you can't give this person another thought. He is not worthy of being your enemy.

The minute you get successful, people will be gunning for you. When I started my company and had no money, everyone was rooting for me. When my business took off, many of those cheerleaders turned on me. Some even hit below the belt by telling lies that hurt my reputation. It's the price you pay for success.

You're going to get negative Google and Yelp reviews. Even when you do nothing wrong, people will report you to a consumer protection agency and the Better Business Bureau. They'll file false unemployment claims. What do all these people have in common? They all exist in your rearview mirror. These are annoyances that don't deserve to be dignified with the word "enemy."

An ex-spouse who is constantly gaslighting you creates a challenge.

You are probably this person's enemy, and they won't ever stop trying to drag you into battles. Don't take the bait. If you don't have kids with this person, avoid them at all costs.

If you do have kids, it will be hard to avoid getting pulled into their drama. If you're a short-term thinker, you may be tempted to go to war with your ex and show your kids that you're the "better" parent. If you're a long-term thinker, you will take the high road, swallow your ego, and show respect to this person—especially because your kids are always watching. Making an ex-spouse your enemy will create a negative impact on both you and your kids. Doing so publicly, as Kanye West learned the hard way, is an even bigger mistake. Whether you are right or wrong, letting the press know about your divorce can only make you look bad and create distractions for your business.

Choose enemies that give you energy, not drain your energy.

5 Unworthy Enemies

1. Companies trailing you in the marketplace
2. People you have surpassed in your business or on your career path
3. Relatives who put you down because they are jealous of your success
4. Toxic people who try to pick fights and bring out the worst in you
5. Small thinkers with a victim mentality

IDENTIFY ALL THE COMPETITORS
AND UNDERESTIMATE NONE

Now that we know who to choose (and who to skip) as our enemies, let's shift from enemy to competition and build the logical block. Imagine if the Coca-Cola Company thought its only competitors were PepsiCo and Keurig Dr Pepper. This would mean its leaders were thinking too narrowly. Since Coca-Cola is in the nonalcoholic beverage industry, they have to look at all threats in that space. Protein drinks, bottled water, and energy drinks were barely part of the picture half a century ago. Now those categories are a huge part of the market.

A threat can be an idea. As sad as it sounds, diabetes education and prevention is a threat to soft drinks. Campaigns to get sugary drinks out of schools are also a threat. Better municipal water combined with a marketing campaign that makes consumers trust their tap water could decrease sales of bottled water. As you can see, threats and competition go hand in hand. Now are you seeing how Coca-Cola has to expand its competitive lens beyond Pepsi and Dr Pepper?

Stop saying you don't have any competition. If you're doing that, you're not thinking about how your customers solve their problems. Imagine saying that you're going to be the only company that has a party bus from Los Angeles to Las Vegas. One, it's hard to see how that would be sustainable, and two, you are also competing with airplanes and cars. If, instead, you identified your competition more broadly, you could figure out how to differentiate your service.

Since many people can't stand airport security, flight delays, and baggage restrictions, we're going to offer a luxury bus with Wi-Fi, high-end TVs, and beverages. This will cost less than a tank of gas and eliminate the hassle of driving. The party will start the minute you step on the bus, and it will be a fun and economical way to get to Vegas with all your stuff.

Your job is to identify the pain points of consumers, and then position yourself to solve those pain points. With a statement like the one written above, instead of pretending you don't have competition, you have devised a strategy to beat them.

For Elon Musk, he's thinking much bigger than a party bus. His Boring Company has already created an underground transit system that links the Las Vegas Convention Center to casinos. His plan is to extend it all the way from Las Vegas to Los Angeles. His competition is air travel, so he needs to make sure his service is priced according to its value. His competition is also regulators and anyone fighting to stop him from building it. The petroleum industry, for example, could be a silent competitor that is lobbying against the transit system.

Ask any mortgage broker what their biggest threat is. It's not the company next door or the online brokers. It's rising interest rates. The same goes for homebuilders, though they have another threat to deal with in supply chain issues. If, for example, a homebuilder can streamline their supply chain by using local suppliers, it will address a threat and get a leg up on their competition.

If you think the only competition for a private secondary school is other private secondary schools, you have blinders on. What about homeschooling, online learning, and a recession? Even ChatGPT is changing the game for schools because it makes information a commodity.

For private colleges, their competition isn't just other private schools and lower-cost public schools. It's also changes in student loan policies, a recession, and, maybe more importantly, a *shift in how people view* education. The moment the narrative shifts and people stop believing that a college degree is required for career success, the value proposition gets destroyed.

Taking a broad view of your competitors doesn't mean stressing out about what could go wrong. It means being deliberate about identifying your competitors to see how they will go after you and poking holes in your own business model. Once you see this, you have to adapt your key differentiators to meet the needs of your customers. For the top universities, online education started out looking like a threat, but once these schools realized they could create their own online courses and degrees, it became an additional revenue source.

Indirect and Unseen Competitors

1. Interest rates
2. Changes in customer behavior
3. Technology that can make you obsolete
4. The economy and economic trends
5. Legislation and lobbyists
6. Companies that meet customer needs in different ways
7. Paradigm shifts that impact your value proposition

THE BEST DETECTIVE IS YOU

When you get better at gaining information about the competition, you make better decisions that minimize risk and increase returns. This is exactly what you, as a business owner or intrapreneur, want to do to improve your odds of longevity. You can hire all the research firms and consultants you want, but the best approach is to research the competition yourself.

When I was selling gym memberships for Bally Total Fitness in my early twenties, I wanted to find out the scripts for my competitors. I would call LA Fitness and 24 Hour Fitness and pretend to be a customer. I would listen to their pitches and take notes. I would then give every objection in the book so I could hear their rebuttals. Again, I took notes and added them to my own list for how to overcome objections.

Once I found out everything I wanted to know about them, I tried to find out everything I could about *my company*. That's when I started calling other Bally gyms as well. It's what marketing firms get paid to do. Since few will do it with the same attention to detail as you, I recommend you start by doing it yourself. Right after hearing how Bally pitched, I would call up my competitors and say, "My girlfriend keeps telling me we should join Bally. She's convinced it's the best gym in town."

That was the perfect way to hear how my competition sold against me. They would list all the bad things about Bally. "They require a contract. People sue them all the time to break their contracts. Their equipment is outdated. They don't have basketball. Their hours are shorter."

I would play right into it. "Yeah," I said, "but they also have a steam room and Jacuzzi, and she says they have the best personal trainers."

Again, I would shut up and listen. They would tell me every bad thing that they tell all their customers about Bally.

So what do you think happened?

When I would sit down with a new prospect, I was already five moves ahead of them. I could say, "I bet the guys at 24 Hour Fitness probably told you dot dot dot." They would look at me like, yeah, that's exactly what they said. And because I knew my competition, I had already rehearsed how I would sell against them.

In the movie *Air*, Sonny Vaccaro (played by Matt Damon) told Michael Jordan's mom, Deloris (played by Viola Davis), exactly what

Converse and Adidas would say in their pitches. He even instructed Mrs. Jordan on what questions to ask that would highlight weaknesses in Converse and Adidas. When those pitches went exactly as Vaccaro described them, he gained a huge advantage. You can only gain this type of edge when you are maniacal about studying the competition.

With social media, your competitors are making it easy for you to study them. Go to their LinkedIn page, their Facebook page, and their websites. It's simple to compare not only prices, but also products and service offerings online. If you're not doing this, you're missing out on ways to win.

The greater the competition, the more research you need to do. And let's not forget about how the enemy ties in here: the more you fear and respect your enemy, the more obsessive you will become about researching your competition. If you're opening a new sports bar, you'd better do more than visit every sports bar in town. Don't just show up once. Go at different times on different days and ask dozens of questions. Tip well and ask the servers and bartenders what nights are slowest. Pay attention to their specials. See how they market themselves on days when there aren't many sporting events. Do all the competitive analysis that you can by yourself, and if you have the budget, also invest in market research.

I've done this for every job I've ever had. When I started with Morgan Stanley in 2001, I'd call Smith Barney and TD Waterhouse and make up a good story. I knew what would qualify me as an ideal prospect, so I would say that I had recently inherited money. Then I would ask, "What's different about you? Why should I trust you with my aunt's hard-earned money?" I would listen and take notes. Then I would say, "My brother has a friend who works at Morgan Stanley, and he thinks we should pick them."

They would start talking, and I would start writing! I wanted to know exactly how they sold against us. And guess what? With my detective skills, they never outsold me again.

Key Questions about Competitors

1. Who are your direct competitors?
2. Who are your indirect competitors?
3. What competitors aren't so obvious but still need to be monitored?
4. Who are you underestimating? The people who get underestimated the most are those without much experience. They have nothing to lose.
5. Where are your opponents strong? What markets/areas will you concede?
6. Where are your opponents weak? What markets/areas will you attack?
7. Who can you acquire? What strategies will you employ to acquire them at the lowest valuation? (Weaken them to drive down the price.)
8. Who could acquire you? What strategies will you employ to get acquired at the highest valuation?

When you can identify the competition, you can devise a strategy to beat them. Make a broad list of competitors and figure out how you differentiate yourself. As you prepare for the upcoming year, and the next two decades, you have to see beyond what currently exists.

USE COMPETITION TO CONSERVE CAPITAL

Now let's look at competition from another angle. When you're planning the upcoming year, as much as you think about growing revenue, you also have to think about containing costs. One of the best ways is to always have several companies bidding on your business. When I delegate anything to my team—whether it's buying computers or office equipment, hiring lawyers, or choosing a convention hotel—they know to always come to me with at least three options.

Why do you think used car salesmen are always pushing you to buy *today?* Because if you studied the competition, you would find a better price. If you took it to the next level and solicited multiple bids, you could pit each dealer against each other. In doing so, you gain control and get the best deal. And when you stop doing this, especially with lawyers and consultants, you end up leaking a lot of money.

In a mastermind that I led, I was talking to an entrepreneur who kept getting calls from private equity companies looking to invest capital in him. He has a solar business doing $70 million a year, with $10 million in EBITDA (earnings before interest, taxes, depreciation, and amortization, which is the "bottom line" number most investors want to know). It was no surprise why private equity companies wanted a piece of him. I asked, "Have you ever raised money before?"

He told me no. This was all foreign to him. I warned him that even though companies are courting him, it wouldn't be long before they started bullying him with unfavorable terms. They would ask for as much equity as possible and create more ways to control him. The key word is control. Whether it's by demanding board sets or out-lawyering him with clauses in the agreement, he was going to be facing vultures who presented themselves as allies.

The way to fight back was with knowledge, specifically research about the competitors in this space. I told him to go online and find out what the last ten solar companies sold for. Then see who sold/brokered the deals, and who bought them.

If you find your business in a similar situation, it's easy to search for a company who represents a seller. It's probably a big company like Goldman Sachs, UBS, or JPMorgan Chase. Call those investment bankers. Here's the script: "Is this John Doe? Great. I noticed you sold XYX for $X. I run a solar company. Our revenue is $X and our EBITDA is $Y. I'm on the Inc. 5000. I'm being approached by other buyers and investors. Before I choose to partner with one of them, I thought it best to do my own research to see what the market will say. What are investors interested in today? What's important to them? What do they value the most? Is it just EBITDA? Is it technology? Is it markets others are not in? What does the market landscape look like? Do you do deals like this? What's your fee structure?"

Then call at least three other investment bankers. Just as I was ahead of people when I sold gym memberships because of the research I did, you'll gain the same advantage. "It's interesting you say that. I just spoke to John over at Goldman. They were the ones who sold ABC. They told me that their structure is dot dot dot."

Now they know you've done your homework; they have to get more *competitive*. You will get the best deal from your investors and negotiate the best terms by making them aware that you are studying their competition.

As you plan for the upcoming year, do an audit of all your expenses. For anything above $1,000, make sure you are getting at least two bids. If it's over $5,000, three bids, and if it's over $25,000, four bids. This is especially important for all your service providers like IT consultants, insurance companies, and attorneys. Tell them exactly what you're doing. You'll find out quickly that their prices change when they know you are shopping their competition.

KEEP FINDING NEW ENEMIES

By now, you may be thinking I'm cutthroat. And if you're a psycho-competitor, you're loving this. You're not going to find this in any other books. This is not *Chicken Soup for the Soul*. If you can recruit an enemy that makes you emotional, I feel sorry for that enemy!

Enemies are the solution to laziness. I guarantee you that if you have the right enemies that create the right emotions, you can't be lazy. How long would you let somebody offend your wife in front of you before you reacted? Do you need a week? A month? What if you're tired at that moment? Will it stop you from taking action?

I never stop looking for people who drive me. Each year I identify at least one specific enemy. I've got stories for days about enemies who motivated me:

- A public hospital administrator who shamed me when my dad got sick. She wouldn't attend to my dad when he needed her after another heart attack.
- A company that didn't listen to my suggestions and basically told me to "shut up and sell."
- A company that sued me when I started my own company.
- My high school guidance counselor, Ms. K., who said, "I feel sorry for your parents. If I was your parent, I'd also have heart attacks. You've brought a lot of pressure on them."

Let me remind you that all my stories are to get you to think about your own life. Take a moment to think of at least three enemies in your life. I don't want you to be a spectator in this process.

When I was twenty-five, I felt like I was moving in the right direction. After my dad had been shamed at the Christmas Eve party, I used the fuel from that enemy to gain knowledge and momentum. Since my

Expedition got repossessed, I was driving a Ford Focus without power windows. As I started to make some money, I was no longer drowning in debt and worrying about paying my bills. I was successful enough that I could relax a little. There was some comfort in not being broke, but I could also see that I was getting *too* comfortable. Based on the last quarter of the year, I had hit a plateau. There was nothing to indicate that my next year would be any better.

Just as I am advising you to do, I had to choose a new enemy. Those men at the party no longer riled me up. The wound that had once been so raw had mostly closed. That's when I realized that I needed a new enemy. Let's call him Harry. He was a direct competitor to the firm I was in.

Harry was known for being disrespectful, and I didn't like the way he spoke to the people who reported to him. You can spot two trends here. First, I don't like bullies who abuse power. Second, as you saw from the men who belittled my dad at the Christmas Eve party, I am territorial. I can't stand people who offend my family and colleagues.

Harry was one of the highest earners in my industry, had a beautiful wife, and was also making big bucks as a motivational speaker. **Sometimes God will put a Goliath in front of you to bring out the David in you.** When my Goliath didn't appear, I went looking for him.

I found out about a big convention in Phoenix where Harry was speaking. I got into my Ford Focus and drove six hours through the desert so I could hear what he had to say. Harry may have known who I was, but he didn't think I was in his league. I was too much of an amateur back then to be a worthy competitor. The fact that I felt as if Harry disrespected me was all in my head. Take that as guidance; your enemy doesn't even have to know they are your enemy.

Harry was making $2 million a year and living in a $4 million house. His speech was sick. He knew how to use emotion to sell the dream, and he was detailed enough to outline a logical path. He wasn't a millionaire by accident. So, of course, everyone was kissing this guy's ass. After the speech, I fought through a group of people until I was face-to-face with him, and, as if I were possessed, I said to him, "I'm going to build a business ten times bigger than yours, and you will never be able to compete with me on my level."

A confrontational approach isn't for everyone. In fact, in the book *The Art of War*, Sun Tzu says, "Never wake up an enemy." But for me, I was trying to *wake myself up*. The right enemy will do something for your business that all the capital in the world can't. If you find the right enemy, it could be worth millions, if not more. I didn't have a shred of evidence to show that I could succeed, but I had fire in my eyes, and I confronted Harry.

He flipped. Security started inching closer to us. Everyone around us thought we were going to fight. I wasn't going to throw a punch, but I was prepared to protect myself. I braced for impact. To the relief of security, Harry attacked only with words. He called me every name in the book. Those insults didn't really sting, but then he got specific. "Bet-David, you're full of shit. You're not willing to work as hard as me. You're not as focused as me. You're not as great of a leader as me. And you never will be."

I looked him straight in the eye and said, "Thanks, buddy. That's the exact message I drove six hours to hear."

Harry looked as confused as the group that had gathered around us. Those looking for a fight didn't get their wish, but I sure did. Right after I thanked Harry, I took a deep breath and thought to myself, *That was exactly what I needed to hear. He said things that were true that others had been afraid to say. What a gift. Now we are going to war.*

This approach may sound extreme. It *is* extreme. But this is a book written for the audacious few. It's not for the cautious majority.

Immediately after this confrontation, I went on a massive run. I thought about Harry many times a day. I printed out his words and laminated them: "Bet-David, you're full of shit. You're not willing to work as hard as me. You're not as focused as me. You're not as great of a leader as me. And you never will be."

If you're going to use your enemy to create emotion, do everything you can to bring it to life. Sports teams are always looking for "locker-room material." Any bad word uttered by an opponent gets printed and placed on the bulletin board or written on the chalkboard. It could be a voodoo doll or a picture to put on your dart board. The goal isn't to be ridiculous; it's to find ways to keep that enemy top of mind and in your face—until you graduate to the next enemy.

I keep a list of all the bad things people have ever said about me. I pull it up in my mind all the time. As if commanded by Sun Tzu, I keep my friends close, and my enemies closer.

GRADUATING TO NEW ENEMIES

Years later, Harry got in trouble with the SEC and took a hard fall. And honestly, I was upset about it. For one, I didn't hate him as a person. And two, I missed competing against him. When I heard about Harry's demise, did I rub it in his face? Of course not. If I did, that would only show that I was making the same mistake that Harry had made: choosing the wrong enemy.

When I led my first public workshop on business planning at the end of 2021, there were mixed reactions at first. When I got emotional, some of the buttoned-up CEOs thought I had lost my mind. Then, during the Q&A, every question and comment was about enemies. People were crying. Emotions poured out whenever they spoke about their enemies. For the rest of the year, business owners and sales leaders were calling me to tell me how focusing on their enemy created exponential growth.

One of the CEOs I mentor had grown his business from $10 million in annual revenue in 2016 to more than $40 million by 2020. Let's call him Pablo. He came to the workshop because, in 2021, he had hit a plateau. The problem is when you scale a business, you take on more overhead. So when growth was flat in 2021, he barely made any profit.

As you can guess by now, I kept asking Pablo about his enemies. It turned out that his daughter had married a man whose father had bullied him growing up. Instead of bonding over the marriage of their kids, this man kept punking Pablo. The guy was barely making a living, so it was obvious to any outsider that he was driven by envy. But emotions aren't logical! For Pablo, all the childhood traumas came flooding back to him, and it distracted him from the business. It became a chain reaction that impacted him at work and at home. Instead of focusing on a worthy enemy, Pablo became distracted by an unhealthy obsession.

It only took me asking Pablo a few questions for him to see his problem. He hadn't graduated to a new enemy. He was dominating his local market. He was making more money than he had ever imagined. Enemies had fueled him on his way up, and the fear of not being good enough turned him into a warrior. Subconsciously, he went looking for a new enemy.

Pablo's mistake was choosing the wrong enemy. He started fighting a guy that he had already beaten. Wanting to get revenge on a guy who wasn't a worthy competitor wasn't going to get him anywhere. To graduate to a bigger enemy, you have to let go of enemies who don't deserve your energy. If you dwell on an enemy you have already beaten, you can't slay the next dragon.

For Pablo, once he identified his new enemy, a regional competitor that had been stealing his market share and had better technology than him, he knew exactly how and where to direct his efforts. His systems and culture building blocks were weak. He had his own skill gaps to address, including conflict resolution. He left the workshop with a list of books to read. Clarity of enemy redirected his focus. That created a positive ripple effect. With his priorities back in order, he was able to mend fences with his childhood bully. As a result, his relationship with his daughter improved, and he was on his way to building a happy extended family.

Let this be a cautionary tale: Pablo's business could have very easily unraveled if he had continued to choose his enemies *un*wisely.

WHEN YOU'RE UP AGAINST IT, CALL ON YOUR ENEMIES

Your enemy is also your competition, but your competition may not always be your enemy. In fact, when you don't have an emotional charge against a competitor, that might make you complacent. When you do have a charge, you find strength that you didn't know you had.

In 2011, I was lying in bed next to my wife, Jennifer. My business had been around for two years, and just when I thought we had crawled our way out of despair, I got a call with some bad news. This person told me, "North American is going to drop your contract in thirty days." They were our biggest insurance carrier, a $40 billion company. Without a carrier, we didn't have a product to sell. Without a product to sell, we didn't have a business. Things looked pretty bleak.

My competitors were out for blood. They got ahead of me and started calling other carriers, telling them I was going out of business and not to work with me. Word on the street spread that I was about to go bankrupt. Sadly, the rumors were true. I can say all this now, but at the time, we couldn't show any weakness or let anyone know we were running out of money.

I couldn't blame North American for wanting to drop us. We were weak on too many of the building blocks. We didn't have the technology, the infrastructure, or the systems. I wasn't qualified to be a CEO.

I talked to the president of North American, Garth, and pleaded with him to keep the contract. I told him the truth, that I didn't have any other options and would be forced out of business. Garth showed some empathy, but he was looking out for his business, not for me, and he remained unconvinced. North American dropped us. But even with all this turmoil, I knew we had to show strength.

Jennifer had married me knowing that I could have easily sustained a multi-seven-figure income if I had stayed with my former company as a sales leader. Instead, I had $13,000 to my name and everything going against me. People were calling her to tell her what a mistake I had made—and they had plenty of evidence to support that claim.

I came home at midnight from the office with her in bed crying because she just had a miscarriage. She was doing her best to keep it together, but all the pressure was a lot to bear. It was getting to both of us. What made it even worse is that I felt like it was all my fault that this was happening. If I hadn't left my job and started a company, our lives would have been far more peaceful.

It was 1:30 a.m. when Jen finally fell asleep, and I walked outside. We lived in an apartment complex called the Summit. I grabbed my iPod and turned on Foreigner's "I Want to Know What Love Is" because it took me back to my military days. Plus, I literally wanted to know what love was in the insurance industry because I didn't have any of it at that time.

As I walked, I prayed and spoke to God. I asked, "Why is this happening?" I felt like I was doing all the right things. I was working a hundred hours a week. I was reading. I was driving my team. I was leading. I kept asking God, "Why did this happen to us?"

Looking back, I realized that I sounded like a victim, which didn't serve me in any way. I'm not asking you to feel sorry for me. I'm warning you that, if you have a big vision, you will encounter moments like this many times. You'll be faced with decisions that will feel like life and death. This is part of the price we have to pay to do something big. Again, that's why this book is only for the audacious few.

I didn't sleep that night. All I thought about was everyone who had doubted me, bullied me, shamed me, and badmouthed me. I can tell you a couple of their names and what they said:

> **Barney:** "You won't make it. You don't have the experience of running an insurance agency."

> **Edgar:** "You will fail and file bankruptcy. You're a phony company."

As I lay in bed, all I could think about were these enemies. Edgar had called everyone in the industry to spread the rumor that we were going out of business. He had also created burner accounts and would go around trashing me until one time he didn't switch over his accounts on Facebook and we realized it was him. Edgar quickly deleted the message and said it was his assistant, who had his phone. Even while it was happening, I knew it was all a game and saw it as a sign of weakness. In fact, it gave me confidence to know that Goliath was scared of David. Not to mention that if I had thrown in the towel, Edgar and the rest of my doubters would have been right about me. I had too much pride to give them that satisfaction.

When Jen woke up, I still hadn't been able to calm myself down. Knowing that neither of us were in the best state, I asked, "Do you think we made the right decision to start the company?"

She looked at me and could see the pressure weighing on me. After a few seconds, she said, "Whatever you do, babe, I got your back."

I realized in that moment that, for all my faults and mistakes, I had done two things right. I had chosen my enemies wisely, and I had chosen my life partner wisely. The enemies propelled me, and my wife supported me.

I also realized that there wasn't time to feel sorry for myself and act like a victim. The next day, I called everybody and anybody I knew. I uncovered possibilities that I didn't know existed. Before that day, I wouldn't have considered doing business with AIG because they needed three months of premiums in advance.

But with my back against the wall, I called AIG. My only request was for them to look me in the eye before saying no. When they agreed, I immediately flew out to Houston, Texas. In 2011, AIG had plenty of enemies as well. In fact, AIG was the most hated company in America then. They barely stayed in business after the financial crisis.

I'll never forget sitting in that room in Houston with twenty people around the table. Here I was, a guy who had barely graduated from high school, in a boardroom filled with lawyers and compliance executives, using every ounce of both emotion and logic to sell them on why it was safe to do business with me. They grilled me nonstop, asking questions left and right. Some of the people in the room were convinced. Others looked as if they couldn't wait for me to leave. I didn't waver. The stakes were too high for me to let up. It took nearly three hours before they said they would even consider giving me a contract.

They needed us, and we needed them. We were united by our desire to prove our enemies wrong. I continued to sell them, and finally they agreed. We got the contract and saved the business. My company's unsung hero was Edgar, our enemy. He may have hurt us in the short-term, but in the long-term, he made us tougher than nails.

Nine years later, North American came to recruit us. Did we turn our nose up and tell them no?

That's ego. That's foolish pride. That's not good business. We said yes. They were never our enemy. They were just a smart company that was the catalyst for me to leverage my enemies and find a gear I didn't know I had. Even though it ended poorly the first time around, we now have a great relationship with them.

COMPASSION FOR YOUR ENEMIES

By now you understand how to choose your enemies and the importance of graduating to new enemies. People like Edgar and Harry were great motivators at the time, but once they served their purpose, I stopped letting them occupy real estate in my mind. As our friend Pablo learned, enemies are healthy. Grudges are not.

None of my enemies that drove me when I first started in business drive me anymore. I now appreciate them as competitors because they keep fighting. I have tremendous respect for anyone who's willing to get in the arena. Whether it's dirty or fair, I'm a big boy. I understand the game.

I don't believe in kicking people when they're down. In a sales contest, you can run up the score and call out your teammates. That's all part of a healthy competitive culture. But you also don't cross certain lines.

After Harry got in trouble, he spread awful rumors about me. I had graduated to new enemies, but for him, I was enemy number one. Then, out of the blue one night, Harry called me right before midnight. I could tell he was crying. Harry confessed how broken he was when he lost ten of his brokers and got in trouble with the SEC. I listened and did my best to comfort him. We agreed to meet at Denny's, and I treated him like a human being, not an enemy.

In the UFC, guys talk trash to each other. They fight until the death, and then when it's all over, they hug. There is mutual respect between people who put their bodies and pride on the line in front of millions of people. That's why I'm willing to help any entrepreneur who goes through tough times. I can put the past aside, and one man to another, do my best to help him out.

I gave Harry a CD of a sermon from my pastor, Dudley Rutherford, which I thought would give him the right perspective to deal with adversity. An hour later, at 2:30 in the morning, Harry called me again in tears. He told me how much he needed to hear this message. I respect and understand the pain of building a business, which is why I was there to support him.

Don't be surprised if your enemies come back to you. You know that expression, "Hustle until your haters ask if you're hiring." It's happened to me dozens of times, and I've hired many of them. Some of my enemies even became allies who helped me fight bigger enemies. And that can only happen if you treat your enemies with the compassion and mutual respect the moment calls for.

ABOVE ALL ELSE, CHOOSE WISELY

We have covered a lot of ground in this chapter. When most people start out in business, they can identify their enemies. It forces them to find another gear and they start to win. Then for the cautious majority, complacency kicks in. When I see that happen, when there's no longer any fire, people start to plateau. More often than not, a fall is on its way. That's what happens if you don't replace old enemies with new ones. Just as a boxer graduates to tougher opponents, you must keep graduating to new enemies.

Enemies are emotional. Studying competition is the logical building block and will play a big role in your success. You have seen how to do the research yourself and go beyond the surface. Take a broad view of your competitors and assume they wake up every day with the goal of putting you out of business.

Studying the competition and choosing the right enemies will continue as long as you care to have a business. Choose wisely.

YOUR BLOCKS

ENEMY

Actions:

1. Go back through your life to identify your enemies. The ones who produce the most emotion get the highest grades.

2. Write out specifically what was said by an enemy that stung the most. The look. The smirk. The more details, the better.

3. Pick a specific enemy for this year, season, or campaign. Name at least one for you personally and one for your business.

4. Remove any unworthy enemies. Check your ego. Identify who you're holding a grudge against or who is below you now and let them go.

5. Decide right now how you will celebrate when you defeat your enemies.

COMPETITION

Actions:

1. Who are your direct competitors? Who are your indirect competitors?

2. Make a list of other *solutions* that compete to meet the needs of your current and prospective customers.

3. Ask the right questions and identify the competition that doesn't yet exist.

4. Become a detective and study your competitors to see how they position themselves against you. Watch how they answer calls and email requests. Study their social media and their websites. Analyze their approach to learn your own weaknesses and how to differentiate yourself from them.

5. Go through expenses and make sure you are getting multiple bids on all your products and services.

CHAPTER 5

Will and Skill

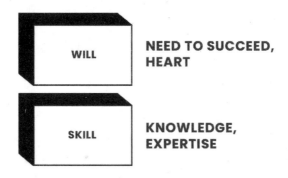

You have to train your mind to be stronger than your feelings or else you will lose yourself.

Mike Tyson

love stories. That's why I read so much and watch so many movies. One of my all-time favorite movie scenes is from *The Dark Knight Rises*, the 2012 film directed by Christopher Nolan, in which Christian Bale plays Batman.

Batman has tried to escape from prison several times, always with a rope, and has failed every time. He's ready to give up when a blind prisoner says to him, "How can you move faster than possible, fight longer than possible, without the most powerful impulse of the spirit: the fear of death?"

Batman says, "I do fear death. I fear dying in here, while my city burns, and there's no one there to save it."

"Then make the climb," the blind prisoner says.

"How?"

"As the child did. Without the rope. Then fear will find you again."

I don't have to tell you what happens next. It's a movie, but even so, it fires me up every time I watch this clip. To me, this was art imitating life. Was the other prisoner speaking logically? Did he use a PowerPoint presentation with spreadsheets and a list of pros and cons to inspire Batman?

Of course not. So why do you think that's the only way to operate a business? Why are you so quick to abandon emotion in the boardroom or the sales meeting when it's the fuel that moves us? Take a page from the blind prisoner and find a way to tap into willpower—yours as well as others'. When people are at their lowest point, when they are terrified, they do the impossible.

The f-word (fear) gets a bad rap. Fear can drive you to do whatever it takes. You need to make two sales to hit your quota? Big deal. What happens if you need two sales to pay for life-saving surgery for your kid?

Fear is often an easy way to help you tap into will, though it's not the only part of what we also call "will." Will is defined as "the mental faculty by which one deliberately chooses or decides upon a course of action."

Will is emotional. It's wanting something in a way that you can't describe. Skills are logical. They are the tools that allow you to impose your will in a way so that you win. As we will do for all the building blocks, we'll integrate will and skill to keep building your plan.

Wanting success is crucial. But it's not enough. In sales, for example, you need to know how to build rapport, ask questions, uncover needs, overcome objections, negotiate terms, and close the deal. Without these skills, all the will in the world will be wasted. After I read Robert Greene's *33 Strategies of War*, I bought the audiobook, and for two years, I kept it on repeat while I was driving. I probably listened to it a hundred times from beginning to end. My will to win led me to work on the skills required to win.

In *The Dark Knight Rises*, for Batman to increase his odds of escape, what skills did he need to develop? Strength, balance, and stamina come to mind. The next question is, What must he do to develop those skills?

To fill in the next two building blocks, I want you to ask yourself two questions: What makes you want success so bad? And what skills must you add to achieve this type of success?

WHAT YOU WILL LEARN IN THIS CHAPTER

Money can only move you so far. If your motivation is solely money, you'll stop at some point. You'll become lazy or complacent. If you want to do something big with your life, you have to tap into something more powerful than wealth.

The ones who keep fighting are driven by something much bigger. Call it an indomitable spirit, determination, purposeful action, or, as we'll say in this chapter, *will*. Enemies light the match. Will keeps the fire burning.

Some questions to ask yourself as we continue:

* Where does **will** come from?
* Why **must** you succeed?
* What does it mean to have "**heart**"?
* How can I **push past limitations**?

You understand what it means to have the drive. But you also need the know-how. As you'll see, will and skill go hand in hand. When I had Neil deGrasse Tyson, the famed astrophysicist and author, on my podcast, I asked him about the indicators of success. He said, "To get mathematical on you, why don't we think of each of these features of a person as dimensions on a hypercube." Then he listed the four features:

- Grades
- Social skills
- Ambition
- Capacity to recover from failure

The first two indicate skills. The second two indicate will. The first two can be improved by studying and skill-building. That doesn't mean the second two can't also be improved. In my case, at different points in my life, I lacked both ambition and the capacity to recover from failure. It took an enemy to change my ambition and my ability to recover from failure. As you work through these building blocks, focus on how you can build both skill and will.

WILLPOWER, NOT WANTPOWER

The story of how Pastor Dudley Rutherford built his church, Shepherd of the Hills in Los Angeles, still moves me. When it was just beginning, Pastor Rutherford's church hosted a "101 Class" for new members. Each week, every person was welcomed into the parish through this orientation. Unbeknownst to these new members, the following week, every single person who attended the 101 Class would get a knock on the door. But this wasn't a simple house call from a friendly fellow parishioner, or even someone selected from a welcoming committee. When these new members opened the door, they found themselves standing face-to-face with Pastor Rutherford himself.

Pastor Rutherford visited *every single new member* and introduced himself. He did this until his congregation reached ten thousand members.

Did you catch that? The first *ten thousand* members. I didn't believe it myself. I asked him what would happen if he got forty new members in one week. He said he would create a schedule, map it out, and greet each new member with a gift basket.

He did this for ten years. Is it any wonder he has one of the biggest churches in L.A.? Which word do you think you're not going to find in his vocabulary?

Want.

Want doesn't get you to knock on doors for ten years, long after you have "made it."

Will, on the other hand, means you never stop.

WILL CAN BE LEARNED

When you have will, you don't need motivation. This is why I actively teach will to my team and to my kids. People have this perception that will is innate, that it can't be taught. So how do you explain an under-performing player or a sales rep changing teams and suddenly turning into a killer? I mentioned Sheena and Matt Sapaula earlier. Matt was a marine with the charisma, work ethic, and leadership skills to be a huge earner. Financial services seemed like an ideal industry for him. Even so, for fifteen years, he struggled. Then, when he joined my firm, he caught fire. In addition to building a huge business with his wife, Sheena, Matt built his own brand as the MoneySmartGuy and wrote a book called *Faith-Made Millionaire.*

The will was always there for Matt to reach his potential. He just needed the right culture and the right enemies to bring out the best in him. Because I've seen enough people excel under new leadership, it's worth making the effort to *elicit* will. This goes for both business and parenting.

When my son Dylan was eight, he became passionate about jujitsu. He kept getting better and building confidence. One day, when we were doing some drills, he said to me, "Daddy, I will be the greatest fighter in the world."

I looked him in the eye and asked, "What'd you say?"

When I heard my son say that without any prompting from me, I got fired up, especially since none of my kids had ever said anything like that before.

He said, "Daddy, I will be the greatest fighter in the world."

I said, "Say it one more time. Say 'I will be the greatest fighter in the world.'"

"I will, Daddy. I will be the greatest fighter in the world."

I didn't want this moment to go to waste. We went for a walk, and he said it again. We talked about what it will take, how he will need to train, and what this declaration will require of him. Again, he said, "I will be the greatest fighter in the world."

About two weeks after Dylan's declaration, I picked him up from jujitsu practice. His instructor mentioned that Dylan seemed to have lost interest and his work ethic wasn't what it used to be. At dinner that night, I said, "Dylan, what happened today at practice? Didn't you say you *will* be the greatest fighter in the world?"

The first thing out of his mouth was "I never said that."

I had seen this movie a hundred times. I knew exactly what Dylan was doing, and I wasn't going to let the moment go to waste. "Dylan, you said you *will* be the greatest fighter of all time."

"No, Daddy, I said I *want* to be the greatest fighter of all time."

My wife shot me a look I know all too well. It's the "babe, let this one go" look. But then Dylan's siblings got into it, and there was a consensus that Dylan had said it.

"We all heard you say *will*," I said. "You didn't say *want*. There's a big difference. I'm not going to let you say stuff like that."

Dylan kept digging in. "I said I *want* to be the greatest fighter in the world. I never said I will be the greatest. I said, I want to be the greatest fighter."

Sometimes, as a leader and a parent, you have to know when to both praise and challenge publicly and privately. As long as we sat at that table, Dylan was going to keep digging a bigger hole for himself. I took him by the hand, grabbed the dogs, and headed outside for a walk.

I said to him, "Dylie, I've said stuff like that before, but then I'd get scared. Are you scared?"

Finally, he let his guard down and admitted to being scared. I changed my tone and calmly said, "Tell me why you changed it from *will* to *want*?"

He said, "Because, Daddy, if I say *will*, I have to do it, but if I say *want*, I don't have to do it."

This eight-year-old kid broke down. He was crying on the outside, and I was bawling on the inside. I was so proud. What took me four decades to figure out, my son figured out at eight years old. He figured out the difference between will and want. No one ever achieved anything with *want*power.

How many people say, "I want to be pampered for the rest of my life"? No one cares. "I want to be rich so I can retire my parents." Weak. "I want to travel around the world." Join the club. "I want to have a mansion on a corner lot." So does everyone else who doesn't have one. The word "want" has zero weight behind it.

Want and will start with the same letter and have the same number of letters. One has incredible power. The other has no power.

A lot of people forget that Ray Kroc didn't discover McDonald's until he was fifty-eight. In one of my favorite business movies, *The Founder*, you could see people laughing at Kroc's ideas for decades. But through all his failures, he was making big declarations and fighting to make them true. I wasn't there to record his words, but you can bet Ray Kroc didn't say, "I *want* to build an iconic American business." He said *will*.

Going forward, there's no place for your wants. Imagine for a moment that, no matter how bold an idea, you knew you couldn't fail, and no one could hear this thought but you: What would you declare?

If you're committed to your vision, tell me what you *will* do.

DIG INTO YOUR PAST TO FIND WILL

Some of you are great at writing down your goals but always seem to get stuck. Progress comes from radical transparency and accountability. When you hit a plateau or get stuck, it's because of a limiting belief or not taking 100 percent responsibility. Very few can break through limiting beliefs by themselves. You're going to need a special leader, counselor, or therapist. I needed someone in my life to help me through, and thankfully, I found Pastor Dudley Rutherford. My work with him was very personal and very profound.

The key is the ability to set your ego aside and be open to receive. If you can do this, the results will be life-changing for you and your entire lineage as your willpower increases exponentially.

Again, this comes back to will. The moment you say "never again" may be the moment that everything changes. Without building your skills, it also may not be enough. The skill is being vulnerable enough to admit you need help in the first place. For your business plan to work, you have to get to the root of your issues. You identify them so you can address them. Skill-building means anything that contributes to your life, whether it's joining a gym or starting marriage counseling. Yes, in your building block for skill, I want you to write down the exact actions you must take to overcome your weaknesses, whether they are related more to your business or your life. **When you improve, your business improves.**

Building skills is putting will into action. It's saying yes to getting better. I've heard every excuse in the book for saying no to investing in skills. Too expensive. Not enough time. Too far away. They're all valid—assuming you want to stay where you are. I mentor an entrepreneur and sales executive named Marlene Gaytan, who came from a working-class family. Since college wasn't an option, she started working in sales at age nineteen. She and her coworkers weren't on salary, so it came as a shock when the boss said they had to attend a Tony Robbins seminar—and pay for it themselves. Marlene panicked at first, and then she did something smart. *She looked around.* The complainers didn't stop bitching. The winners bought tickets. Since Marlene knew who she wanted to be, she found a way to dig up the money. In her first year in the business, without a college degree, she made $100,000.

I recently asked Marlene what she learned at the conference. She said, "I honestly don't remember anything Tony Robbins said. I was just so proud of myself that I came up with the money and went. I proved to myself that for the first time in my life, I was serious about my own success. *It completely changed my identity.*"

Did you catch that? **Investing in skills changed her identity.**

Before she turned thirty, Marlene became a millionaire. Together with her husband, Jose, they now run a $40-million-a-year business. Her success reversed a family tradition of thinking small. Marlene did it with a combination of will and skill. It started with desire and continued because she acted on that desire to keep building skills.

PATRICK BET-DAVID with GREG DINKIN

She designed a plan for her life that she would never have believed before.

KEEP DEVELOPING SKILLS TO STAY RELEVANT

According to the *Harvard Business Review*, only 29 percent of new hires have all the skills required for their current roles, let alone future ones. What skill sets do you need to make this *your* year? If you're working in technology or if you're an engineer, falling behind is even more pronounced. As fast as technology moves, you have to keep developing skills or you will become irrelevant quickly. Imagine you are a programmer who only knows how to use C and Pascal. Be prepared for lots of boomer jokes and earning 1995 wages.

You can't back up a declaration without skills. If you start to obsess about a topic, direct that obsession to acquiring more skills. Put your nose in a book or join a mastermind with other talented people.

In 1994, at age thirty-nine, Steve Jobs said, "By the time I'm fifty, everything I've done up until now will be obsolete. This is a field where one does not write a principia which holds up for two hundred years."

One skill we often take for granted is using the internet. But even this skill as we know it could soon become obsolete. As artificial intelligence (AI) continues to develop—and it's moving quicker than you think—you'd better have the skills to utilize it. Peter H. Diamandis, founder of the X Prize Foundation, wrote on his blog, "There will be two kinds of companies at the end of this decade. Those who are fully utilizing AI, and those who are out of business." Ashton Kutcher launched a $240 million AI investment fund in May 2023 and said, "If you're a company and you're sleeping on this, you're probably going to be out of business . . . It's that good and that powerful from a utilization standpoint." These quotes don't sound out of line when you remember that in the mid-1990s, Bill Gates said, "If your business is not on the internet, then your business will be out of business." Fail to build skills quickly, and your passion will go to waste.

Most companies offer training. Others offer reimbursement if you take the initiative to acquire more skills. There are also millions of people who are acquiring critical skills informally on the job or even in their own basements. Gathering new skills is not a question of opportunity. It's all about desire. If you want to learn, you won't have to search hard for how to acquire new skills.

If you don't keep adding skills, you won't be able to compete in the marketplace. Here are three questions to ask to continue constructing your skill block:

1. Who do I need to be to hit next year's forecast?
2. What three to five skill sets are required?
3. What will I commit to for training and personal and professional development?

HOW TO USE BOOKS AND TRAINING TO ADD SKILLS

I can confess to you now that, for years, I was terrible at conflict resolution. The way I improved on that skill is exactly what I'm about to suggest for you. I made it one of my three topics of emphasis and read six books on conflict resolution in one year. Those books included *Leading with Emotional Courage, Difficult Conversations, The Hard Truth about Hard Things*, and, my favorite, *Crucial Conversations: Tools for Talking When Stakes Are High*, which has sold more than five million copies. All this effort, and believe me it was hard, transformed a weakness into a strength.

Instead of immediately setting a goal of reading a certain number of books, first decide what *three skills* you most need to develop next year.

It may be that you are focusing on conflict resolution, negotiation, and integrating AI. Your goal is then to read at least six books on each topic and attend at least one training course on each. By training, it could be a live event, private coach, online course, or mastermind group.

You can make the occasional exception, but for the most part, every book you read and every training course you attend is going to relate to these three skills. **You want to go deep rather than wide.** This allows you to find trends and commonalities. You also want to see contradictions, so you can start to develop your own strategies. This type of commitment does more than undo a weakness. It turns last year's weakness into your future strength.

Building skills starts with you. If accountability is a point of emphasis in your business, you need to start with your own ability to hold people accountable. In doing so, you'll be able to *demonstrate* to your team how to be better at it by constantly modeling the right behavior. If you feel like you need to do more, that's when you bring in an expert to lead a workshop, or maybe you lead the workshop yourself.

The current version of you doesn't have the skills to execute your audacious plan. If you had what it takes right now, you wouldn't need to improve. By identifying three areas of focus and committing to those skills, you are on your way to constructing a rock-solid skill block.

BUILD SKILLS FOR YOU AND YOUR TEAM

Now that we're talking about building your skill block, you may be asking if you need a plan to build your own skills or the skills of people in your organization. The answer is both. If your CFO is brilliant at numbers but puts everyone to sleep during meetings, that impacts the entire company. If your HR director lacks communication skills, you're setting up your organization for burnout, high turnover, or maybe even worse, quiet quitting.

If you're a solopreneur or a person trying to get into business, you only have to think about yourself. If you run a company, you'll work with your team to address their skills. In fact, you are likely already doing so as part of the annual review process. With this business plan, you can integrate those meetings into your plan, which will benefit both you and that individual. At a minimum, ask your direct reports the following:

1. In what three areas did you excel this year?
2. What were three areas that need work?
3. What do you think you need to do in order to address those areas and/or skill deficiencies?

At the beginning of 2022, for my financial services company, we had a kickoff meeting with our VPs as part of an event at the Dallas Cowboys' stadium. We took a survey on what skills we needed to develop, and every one of our vice presidents said that they want to improve conflict resolution. Meanwhile at Valuetainment, we were working on how to improve the communication between content creators, editors, and those on the business side. It was inherently full of conflict, and though we were doing okay, I knew we could improve.

In both my organizations, at the beginning of 2022, I made *Crucial Conversations* the book of the month. For the top leaders, they were required to send me their key insights and then meet to discuss. I then hired a consulting team from Crucial Learning to lead a two-day workshop for both companies. At $30,000 a pop, I spent $60,000 for the two events.

A funny thing happened in the few weeks following these workshops. We had more conflict! On the surface, it was a concern, though we quickly realized that people were now comfortable addressing conflict instead of avoiding it. Cold wars were replaced with real conversations using their new communication skills. The investment paid off for both companies.

Yes, your plan needs to include ways for everyone who impacts your business to add new skills. When you help others win, you win. That's why one of the best things you can do for others is to lead them to invest in skills.

WHOM TO INVEST IN AND HOW TO GET OTHERS TO INVEST IN YOU

I met Maral Keshishian when she was my bank teller at Washington Mutual in Mission Hills, California. I was in my late twenties working as a sales leader, and she was an eighteen-year-old college student at UCLA. I didn't like the way I was being treated and was about to close my account. When I told Maral, she stayed calm, listened, and respectfully said all the right things to win me over. I knew right then that I wanted her on my team. Once I started my own company, I hired her to be our director of finance in 2011.

After she graduated from college, Maral went on to earn an MBA. She also quickly moved up the ranks of my financial services firm. I could write a book about all her strengths, but let's focus on her incredible ability to build skills—and get me to pay for most of them! If you're an intrapreneur or employee, I recommend that you follow her lead. If you're a CEO or an owner, I recommend you invest in people like Maral.

To get others to invest in you, with both time and money, you have to be outstanding at your job and always exhibit integrity. Nothing is worse than a lazy employee who demands more training. Assuming you have proven yourself, here's the formula that Maral perfected.

6 Ways to Get Others to Invest in Your Skills

1. Identify the opportunity (conference, course, event).
2. Write a short description of the return on investment. Focus on how your getting better helps the company.
   a. Potential contacts and revenue opportunities.
   b. Skills that will benefit the firm in the short-term and long-term.
   c. How you become a more valuable asset to the firm.
3. Give alternatives. Your employer is going to be suspicious of your self-interest, especially if the event is in Hawaii or Las Vegas. You gain credibility when you go to them with several options and not just one training or event.
4. Explain how you will keep up with your work while you're gone. This also shows that you know how to delegate and build leaders.
5. While you're at the event, text key learnings and "aha!" moments. Take a picture of a powerful slide and explain how you see this benefiting the company.
6. After the course, send a summary of what you learned, how you're applying it, and the relationships you built. Focus on how the company has benefited, and if possible, give real numbers that justify the investment. Ideally, you can point to closing a deal, but if not, mention the specific opportunities that were created.

I invested $16,000 in sending Maral to Harvard Business School to take executive courses when she was still the director of finance. The decision was easy, since she followed the above six steps in her previous trainings—and kept building skills that helped the firm. She was also constantly asking what her blind spots were, how she could improve, and what books I would recommend. And because she took the advice to heart and kept improving, I kept saying yes to more training.

At age thirty-one, she joined the C-suite as the chief reputation officer. At age thirty-four, she became the firm's president, which made her the youngest woman president in her industry. Maral always had the will, and because she stayed hungry to add more skills, she became part of the audacious few.

MEETINGS REQUIRE SKILL AND WILL

Have you ever been to meetings for traditional insurance companies? Sadly, I've been to more than I care to remember. They have to take all the knives away from people because the meetings are so catastrophically boring. When you go to an insurance meeting, you don't need paper and pencil. You need a pillow.

You do not want to have a reputation for running boring meetings. If you do have this reputation, how can you improve your skill in this area? What action steps must you take to make meetings better? Here is where you start to seamlessly integrate will and skill.

Start with these three questions:

1. Why is this meeting so important?
2. What is my intention?
3. What behavior and attitude do we want people to have after this meeting?

Believe me, the will to have an effective meeting is powerful, because it gets you to spend the time to plan and be skillful in how you set it up, before, during, and after. Seek out those who lead great meetings. Ask them how they prepare. Ask what books they read or what else they did to get better. Then when you're in their meetings, you'll see that they have a formula. Read the *HBR Guide to Making Every Meeting Matter.* Study how Jeff Bezos leads meetings, including these three tips:

3 Rules for Meetings According to Jeff Bezos

1. Keep the group size manageable. Bezos said, "We try to create teams that are no larger than can be fed by two pizzas. We call that the two-pizza team rule."
2. No PowerPoint. Use actual memos that tell stories instead of recite data.
3. Start with silence. Give people time to read the memos or relevant information before starting the discussion.

WHAT TYPE OF WILL IS REQUIRED TO EARN YOUR REPUTATION?

As part of a mastermind that I lead, I was mentoring a couple, Matthew and Hengameh Stanfield, who started a chain of pizza shops. COVID-19 nearly destroyed their business. Like most companies, they had major staffing issues. Matthew said, "Well, Patrick, we're just thinking we go back to school and maybe we do something else like go into real estate. This pizza thing is getting really hard. And, you know, we just want to go do something else."

"What are you talking about?" I asked. "So let me get this straight. You have a recipe that works. You're confident that your product is the best. You have loyal customers. You've been doing this pizza thing for three, four years. Now you want to quit this and go to another industry to learn?"

They told me yes, and I admit, I got emotional. "So when that next thing gets hard, you'll quit that thing. Only cowards quit when things get hard."

The Stanfields have a backbone. They had a solid reputation, and they wanted to protect it. When I challenged them, they fought back. They insisted that they weren't cowards. I asked them to think about what quitting would do to their reputation.

This raises a great question about willpower. Some say you can't teach willpower or you can't create willpower. You already know how I feel about that. This is why I'm always looking for the best ways to *elicit* willpower. You have to know how to poke people. To be effective, sometimes you have to make it hurt. *The best leaders know how to disturb people.* This couple had strong principles and values. When they said, "Well, what do you think we should do?" the conversation changed.

Did the word "coward" elicit their willpower?

My dad has an amazing ability to get under my skin and elicit reactions. His brother, my uncle Johnny, is six feet five and loves math. He was a physicist and would always have a physics book in his hand. At forty-five years old, who the hell reads a physics book? I was also tall and good at math, so naturally everybody compared me to Johnny. They would say, "You're Johnny Junior," and I saw this as a compliment.

Then one day my dad said, "Let me tell you what Johnny's reputation is. His reputation is Mister Seventy Percent. You don't want Johnny's reputation. Anytime Johnny starts something, he takes it all the way to seventy percent. And then he scraps it. The moment it gets hard, he runs away and starts a new project."

I cannot tell you how much that scared the hell out of me to have the reputation of Uncle Johnny. I did not want to be that guy. When I was in high school, my dad would say, "Son, stop being so lazy." It was hard to argue with him when I had a 1.8 GPA.

In my early twenties, I was still trying to find myself. My intensity would come and go. I would work hard to win a contest or hit a monthly goal, but I was more focused on partying. I was on my way to becoming Uncle Johnny.

When I was twenty-four, not long after that humiliating Christmas Eve, I started to get introspective. I wanted to know where all my anger was coming from. What I learned is that my anger came from my own frustration at not being able to make progress on my goals. I thought I was mad at the world, but I realized that I was mostly mad at myself. Unless it was for showing up at the club on time or making it to Vegas twenty-six times a year, I didn't have a solid reputation at the time. And only I was responsible for that.

I told myself, I *will* have a reputation as someone who keeps his word. This would be critical to my business philosophy. When I say I'll do something, I want people to know they can bank on it. When Pat says something's going to get done, it's going to get done, period.

Ask yourself the hard question about what your reputation is—in the marketplace, with your friends, and with your family. Be honest. Do you step up when someone questions your will? What words move you? "Coward," "quitter," "winger"? Do you notice a pattern of quitting too soon? Those are questions to reflect on so you can tap into your own will. As I've said, will isn't fixed. When buttons get pushed, we act differently. That's why your job is to figure out how to push your own buttons.

What elicits *your* willpower? What words trigger *you*? Is there likely some truth to them?

Whether you're reading this on January 1 or July 1, this is a chance to start fresh and cement a new reputation. What do your friends say about you? What do your coworkers say about you? What does your family say about you? What does your spouse say about you when he or she lies next to you, and you know they're thinking something about you but they're not telling you what it is? By the way, if three, four, or five people say the same thing about your reputation and they all know you very well, it's probably true.

Are you okay with that? I'm not telling you to go home and fight them. I'm telling you to *earn* the reputation that you want to be known by.

If you ask people what it's like to work with me, they're going to tell you I'm intense. I have high expectations, and I'm nonstop. I'm always going and don't have the best boundaries. If people say that about me, they're not lying to you. That's my reputation.

What three words don't you ever want to hear said about you?

What three words do you want attributed to you?

Once you've figured these out, you can start figuring out what skills you need to build to make the reputation you want for yourself. Once you find your will, you'll learn the corresponding skills.

You can also tie these questions back to your enemies. Think about someone who you don't like saying awful things about you. How fired up does that get you?

For me, because my dad told me about Uncle Johnny's reputation, he elicited the willpower in me that I needed to change this reputation for myself. I declared, I *will* change. I will make it so that everybody who does business with me will say that my word is gold, that if I say I'm going to do something, it will happen.

That declaration, that statement which included the word "will," would never have happened or changed my life if my dad hadn't known exactly how to hit me where it hurt. I don't know anyone who wants to be thought of as Mister Seventy Percent, an underachiever, or a coward. What do you want people to say about you?

RECRUIT OTHERS TO ADDRESS SKILL GAPS

When you get emotional, you must channel it into an action plan that improves your skills. At times, you can do that work yourself. Other times, you can address it by hiring the right people, delegating, or bringing on the right partners.

With the Stanfields, we started talking more about their goal of franchising their pizza business. Neither had any experience in this area. Between them, they were great at making the product and running their stores. It gave them two choices: study everything there is to know about franchising and start paying for legal advice or hire someone who had been there before.

They decided on the second option. They didn't have the bandwidth to learn the franchising game while running the business. This led to the question about skill in recruiting. They asked, "*How* do we recruit who we need?"

We got into the nitty-gritty of recruiting, and I advised them on how to find the best headhunter. For you, it may be that you have to personally recruit, or you may be big enough to have your own internal HR team. The point is, *you either gain the skill or recruit people who have it.*

This couple ended up hiring two former executives from Domino's. Less than a year later, they stood up in front of two thousand entrepreneurs at the Vault (my annual three-day business conference) and shared their story of *expansion.* Not only did they stick with it, but they also grew from four stores to eight with plans to double again in the next year. They made $2 million in the twelve months *after* they had decided to quit.

Why? Because they integrated will and skill. Their story brings to mind that Albert Einstein quote: "It's not that I'm so smart, it's just that I stay with problems longer."

Once their reputation was challenged, they tapped into their will. If they had quit after what I said, they knew they would be in the group known as cowards. And since that word irritated them, in the moment, I became their enemy. That led them to produce the emotion required to activate them toward acquiring skill in franchising, which for them meant recruiting it. They earned my respect, and more importantly, earned a couple of million dollars and set the foundation for a long run.

On the skill side, think about who you need to recruit or what tasks you need to delegate. Let's say you can't stand cooking or grocery shopping and want to eat healthier. It doesn't mean you have to enroll in culinary school or hire a personal chef. What you can do is sign up for a meal delivery service or hire someone for a few hours to do meal prep.

Addressing skill deficiencies doesn't mean doing everything yourself. It's a common mistake to think it's all or nothing. For example, as you expand, you're going to need to put in financial controls. Binary thinkers will say, "My only two choices are to do it all myself or spend a quarter of a million dollars to hire a CFO." The real solution might be hiring a part-time accountant or a fractional CFO, or contracting out your accounts receivable. Maybe one good intern managed by your COO can at least handle the basic functions. Since we don't live in a world of unlimited resources, you need to find ways to plug holes without doing everything yourself.

What skills are crucial to your success that you lack the time, interest, or ability to perform? What's your strategy to bring those skills to your company and/or to your life?

PERFORMANCE VERSUS TRUST: HUMAN SKILLS

I agree with bestselling author Simon Sinek when he says that soft skills should be labeled as *human* skills. With that theme in mind, Sinek made a video about Navy SEALs and how they value their team members when they're going off to war.

Sinek differentiated between trust and performance, which have some similarities to will and skill. In the military, performance is what you do on the battlefield. Trust is who you are off it. In business, performance is about results—revenue, KPIs, tangible metrics. Trust is about integrity—having others' backs and keeping your word.

Who do you value more—somebody you have total trust in or somebody who has a highly specialized skill? What if somebody's an expert, but you don't trust them? What if somebody is trustworthy, but they have no clue what they're doing?

While you're thinking about those answers, take a look at this matrix:

PERFORMANCE vs. TRUST MATRIX

	LOW	AVERAGE	HIGH
HIGH	HIGH PERFORMING LOW TRUST	HIGH PERFORMING MID TRUST	HIGH PERFORMING HIGH TRUST
AVERAGE	MID PERFORMING LOW TRUST	MID PERFORMING MID TRUST	MID PERFORMING HIGH TRUST
LOW	LOW PERFORMING LOW TRUST	LOW PERFORMING MID TRUST	LOW PERFORMING HIGH TRUST

PERFORMANCE (vertical axis)

TRUST (horizontal axis)

Did this matrix make you think about where people on your team fit? Does it make you consider whether you are giving enough credit to trust?

Back in 2011, I identified four people who were at the top of the trust axis but had skill gaps. Their names were Patrick, Maral, Mario, and Tigran. Yes, that Patrick was me—I was at the top of that list! Since I needed to work on leadership and on how to be a better CEO, I enrolled in a leadership course at Harvard. It killed me to step away from the business for a month, but it turned out to be one of the best decisions I ever made. As we discussed before, when Maral joined the C-suite of our company, I sent her to take the same course.

Mario and Tigran were cut from the same cloth. I trusted them completely and their will to succeed was off the charts. Mario started off as the quintessential Ernie. He truly was *willing* to do anything, but when he couldn't execute, both his esteem and the projects he worked on would suffer. Tigran was a talented graphic designer who I saw as a leader. He had strong hard skills, but he needed leadership skills to step into a bigger role. That's why I didn't balk at the tuition price of $12,000 for a marketing course at Wharton Business School. After expenses, I spent close to thirty grand to send Mario and Tigran to Wharton for a week.

I could give you a list of logical reasons why it was a good investment. They learned tangible skills that made them better at their jobs. They brought in new ideas to the company. They networked with high-caliber individuals who forced them to raise their game. What stood out to me most, though, is that, when they returned to the office, they walked differently. Their identity changed. Sure, my investment in them created loyalty, but it was something bigger than that. It was a belief, backed up by a financial investment, that elevated Mario and Tigran beyond anything I could have taught them in the office. Now, both are strong leaders who raise standards and set the tone for our company culture.

I'm in the anticipation business, so I can guess what many of you are going to say. That's a boatload of money! What if those guys leveraged that Wharton credential to get another job? Though I'm tempted to explain why I was willing to take that risk, I'll leave it to two others.

Henry Ford said, "The only thing worse than training your employees and having them leave is not training them and having them stay." And Richard Branson said, "Train people well enough so they can leave; treat them well enough so they don't want to."

What about the highly skilled people you don't trust? If you're saying that you have no choice but to take the good with the bad, this is a sign that an area you need to work on is leadership development. If you believe you are stuck with these people, it means you haven't developed the skills of the people you do trust to do the job. Who do you think Maral, Mario, and Tigran replaced?

I can't go to war with people I don't trust. In some cases, you can put these people in a silo. If it's a software developer, maybe you can give them a project to work on independently. Again, I would be very careful, and if given the choice, I would pick someone with less skill and higher trust.

Trust and personality are different. Let's just say you have a full-on genius of a person who is the best coder but horrible with people. Or you have a CFO who is highly skilled but puts everyone to sleep in his meetings. What do you do with these people?

It depends on how coachable they are. In other words, do they have the *will* to want to get better? If so, make the investment to build their skill block. They might end up becoming some of your most trusted employees. In a perfect world, everyone on your team would rank high in trust and high in skill. Since we don't live in a perfect world, you have to take inventory. The people who you trust the most likely also have the strongest will. If any of those people are low in skills, you must lock on to them. Skills can be taught. Investing in high will/trust people is likely the best investment you can make.

People with strong hard skills and good character turn into reliable citizens who create linear growth for your organization. People with soft skills who experience a paradigm shift become impactful citizens who create exponential growth. Your goal is to create that paradigm shift for a few people, who end up bringing your company to an entirely new level.

THE PARADIGM SHIFT QUADRANT

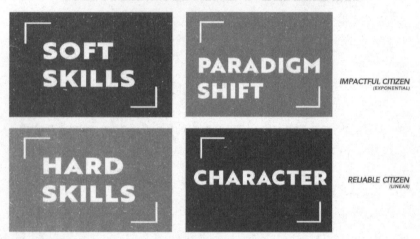

ELICIT WILL AND BUILD YOUR SKILLS

Once you've fully tapped into your will, you are ready to set the world on fire. With this emotion, you feel like you can conquer anything, whether it's the bench press, a pitch deck, or your sales quota. But you also need the skills to do it.

You now understand that will isn't fixed. You can bring it out in yourself and in others. It requires asking the right questions along with the willingness to act urgently when the answers come. Those actions are the ones that help you build the skills required for you to be the person you want to be, which is far different from who you are now.

YOUR BLOCKS

WILL

Actions:

1. What makes you want success so badly? What's your plan to convert *wantpower* to *willpower?*

2. What do you fear most? What thoughts or emotions make you so emotional that you want to do everything in your power to avoid feeling them?

3. What three words don't you ever want to hear said about you?

4. What three words do you want attributed to you?

5. How can you lead in such a way that elicits willpower in others?

6. What patterns and limiting beliefs do you see in yourself, and what will you do (or who will you seek for guidance) to be the one to stop them?

SKILL

Actions:

1. Who do you need to be to hit next year's forecast? What three to five skill sets are required?

2. What type of skills/training will you commit to that has the potential to change your identity?

3. Where do your leaders or team members lack skills? How will you address them?

4. For skills you're not going to address yourself, how will you delegate or who will you recruit?

5. What choices will you make after looking at your Performance vs. Trust Matrix? Who will you invest in and which skills will you emphasize?

6. Fill in the blank: I want my reputation to be defined by the words _____.

7. Fill in the blanks: If I keep having a reputation for _____ (fill in biggest weakness), I won't get to the next level, which will nullify all my hard work. I will address this deficiency by _____.

CHAPTER 6

Mission and Plan

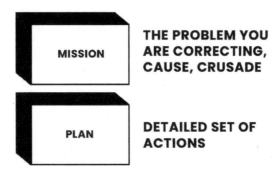

MISSION	**THE PROBLEM YOU ARE CORRECTING, CAUSE, CRUSADE**
PLAN	**DETAILED SET OF ACTIONS**

> A small body of determined spirits fired by an unquenchable faith in their mission can alter the course of history.
>
> **Mahatma Gandhi**

magine a boring CEO at the annual kickoff meeting, reading off PowerPoint slides and walking the team through precise Excel spreadsheets. He is prepared, organized, and specific. He's giving a clinic on how to plan for a successful year, and he has the evidence to back up how the firm will grow revenue and expand into new markets. So why is no one listening?

Now imagine Steve Jobs, in his trademark black turtleneck, blue jeans, and sneakers, standing up in front of his team at Apple, talking about how they are going to change the world. There are no Power-Point slides. The company's mission is etched in his soul. He looks at the crowd and boldly proclaims something like "Our mission is to make a contribution to the world by making tools for the mind that advance humankind."

There's a roar! The crowd goes nuts. They're ready to take over the world.

Why? Because they know their mission—and it's a mission that inspires them.

Jobs can't stop there. Once he has told them *why*, he must next tell them *how*. They are primed to hear and execute whatever plan he lays out.

The logical CEO, on the other hand, has nowhere to go. The minute he lost his audience, there was no getting them back.

By now we understand that emotion and logic must always be intertwined. Not just in every business plan or quarterly meeting, but in every sales call, team huddle, and Zoom call. For the next two building blocks, this couldn't be more true. Mission is highly emotional, and plan is highly logical. Neither is optional.

Having a mission creates endurance. It allows you to tolerate the pain you're going to go through. You don't want to compete with a man or a woman on a mission. You want to *join* someone on a mission. In fact, without a strong mission, you're not going to attract the right people to you. You're just another company to work for, another person solely driven by money. When that's the case, you'll face the constant threat of people leaving you.

WHAT YOU WILL LEARN IN THIS CHAPTER

You will learn how to establish your mission, articulate it, and draw constant inspiration from it. Notice I didn't say *motivation*. When you're on a mission, you don't need motivation. You are driven by the fire from within. And unlike dreams and goals, which we'll cover in later building blocks, your mission does *not* have a timeline. As we dig deeper, you'll see why, for both you and your business, your mission is something that extends beyond one goalpost.

You're also going to learn how to channel that mission into a plan. This will include a SWOT (strengths, weaknesses, opportunities, threats) so you know exactly where to direct your efforts. You will also learn how to anticipate a crisis and always stay three to five moves ahead.

RECRUIT YOUR MISSION

When we're talking about your mission, "recruiting" is an inside job. I use the word "recruit" differently than most. To me, everything is recruiting; it's going out and making things happen, whether it's finding talent for your company or gaining clarity about your mission. With your mission, it's not always right in front of you, which is why you have to recruit it and bring it toward you.

To be more specific about recruiting your mission, there are four things you can do to make it come alive for you.

4 Ways to "Recruit" Your Mission

1. Take the time to see what moves you.
2. Determine what you're sick and tired of.
3. Ask, "What sets me off?"

4. See what bothers you so much that you won't be able to live with yourself if you don't do something about it.

Because it's emotional, there are some parallels to choosing your enemies when figuring out your mission. It may help to think about when you've felt like an underdog or when you felt shame. What is so important that you want to dedicate your life to fixing or improving?

At Valuetainment, we spent years not just thinking about our mission but finding the exact words to articulate it. The mission is to enlighten, empower, and entertain current and future leaders around the world.

Here are excellent examples of mission statements from three very different companies:

- Patagonia: We're in business to save our home planet.
- TED: Spread ideas.
- Tesla: To accelerate the world's transition to sustainable energy.

Here are the personal mission statements of three popular people:

- Oprah Winfrey: "To be a teacher. And to be known for inspiring my students to be more than they thought they could be."
- Walt Disney: "To make people happy."
- Denise Morrison, former CEO of Campbell Soup Company: "To serve as a leader, live a balanced life, and apply ethical principles to make a significant difference."

For all of these companies and individuals, the mission is ongoing. Their plans come from their mission, and though plans have life cycles, the overall mission is never complete.

If you make up a mission statement just to put it on your website, it's a bunch of BS. It won't inspire you. In fact, the people who do that are the ones who are constantly looking for motivation. I've looked at a lot of the literature on writing mission statements. It's mostly tedious stuff that makes writing business plans a chore. Rather than *think* about formulas, I want you to *feel* what actually moves you.

Now is the time to get real about what you really want to do with your life.

Here are a few questions to guide you:

1. What cause are you fighting for?
2. What injustice are you correcting?
3. What crusade are you leading?

Recruiting your mission requires you to get quiet. This is something you do on your own before you get with your team. Turn off your phone and take the time to look inside yourself. Ask these questions and really take the time to discover the answers. It may take a few hours or it may take a few months. It's not something you "search" for. It's something you "allow" to reveal itself. Maybe it's from a part of you that's been hiding, or something you've been denying.

As much as I want to help lead you to your mission, the best I can do is keep giving you the questions to ask and the exercises to try that will help you look inside yourself. One of those exercises comes from a book called *The Leaderless Revolution: How Ordinary People Will Take Power and Change Politics in the 21st Century*, written by a former British diplomat to Iran named Carne Ross. Ross says that the people who start revolutions or do something big or disruptive are those who take action based on three things:

1. What they love
2. What they hate
3. What bothers them

I have painful memories from my childhood, including my parents' divorce and my experiences with communism before our family fled Iran. But don't for a minute think I'm asking for sympathy or calling myself a victim. In fact, it's the scars from manipulation, game-playing, silencing, and communism that led me to *choose the ideological enemies* that created my mission.

When I stopped being angry about my childhood and started reflecting on it, I got closer to discovering my mission. I'll share some more stories in this chapter, but for now I want you to get uncomfortable. What do you hate? What is something you can't stand? Who is getting bullied that you want to stand up for? If it's you or the people close to you, you will really be on to something. Who do you love that needs help? What bothers you produces *juice*. It creates the emotion that you need.

Finding something that bothers you doesn't always have to be this deep or personal. Maybe you love the smell of a clean bathroom or can't stand toxic fragrances. With this thought, a lucrative business may be waiting to be discovered.

Pourri's mission statement is "To delightfully shift the way the world thinks about the things they've always done." According to *Inc.*, it is a $400 million company. Whether this started with founder Suzy Batiz's love of a clean bathroom, hatred of a smelly one, or being bothered by synthetic fragrances, this is a woman who had bankrupted two businesses before connecting to her mission. It also explains why she's not slowing down. Even after making a fortune with the original product, Poo-Pourri, Batiz launched a line of natural cleaning products, because her mission is to shift the way things have always been done.

These examples are for you to continue thinking about your mission. Keep asking these questions: What do you love? What do you hate? What bothers you?

HOW I FOUND MY MISSION

Now that you've seen how others have found their mission, you should be formulating some ideas. In my twenties, I was fueled by proving my enemies wrong, making money, and gaining respect. Looking back, it's pretty normal for people in their twenties to be focused on selfish goals.

In December 2008, six years after the enemies spoke to my dad at that holiday party, all my effort started to pay off. I was doing well for a thirty-year-old. I traveled all over the world. I spoke in front of ten thousand people, and I also spoke at my high school as the inspirational rags-to-riches success story. I also heard the magical words from my parents. You know what those words are: *I'm proud of you.* I believed them, which should have brought peace. So why was I not content? Why was I not fulfilled? Why did I feel like something was missing?

At the end of 2008, I started thinking about the upcoming year and wondering, "Is this all there is to life? All these things I had to go through, were they just to make money? Is this all there is? Why do I need to get out of bed every morning when I'm already wealthier than my wildest dreams?" I knew in my gut that there had to be something bigger than the life I was living. Looking back, I was dancing around the real question: What is my mission?

I tried to rededicate myself. I read motivational books and signed up for motivational workshops. But nothing changed. I couldn't find anything to get me going. Looking back, the one area where I can give myself credit is that I was actively *recruiting* my mission. I asked a lot of questions. I sat down with mentors. I sought the counsel of my pastor, Dudley Rutherford. I asked friends to tell me where my blind spots were.

One of those friends, Bill Vogel, invited me to a meeting at the Miramar Hotel in Santa Monica, California, for the Claremont Institute think tank. It was March 2009, and my year was off to a solid but unspectacular start. I was able to coast and still make good money, which taught me how comfort can be one of life's biggest drags on urgency. I lacked an enemy and a mission, which explains why I felt so directionless.

I pulled up to the Miramar Hotel in my yellow Corvette Z06 wearing a Hugo Boss pin-striped suit. I found myself sitting next to Pat Boone, the famous singer and actor. There were plenty of bigwigs, and none of their speeches did anything to inspire me. I came hoping to get some answers, and I was afraid I was going to leave with none.

Then George Will, a political commentator, author, and Pulitzer Prize winner, stood up to speak. In 1986, the *Wall Street Journal* called Will "perhaps the most powerful journalist in America."

Through three powerful stories, Will started talking about how lawyers are ruining the country. The first was about a frivolous lawsuit from a kid who swallowed a fishhook and sued the manufacturer. The next was about how the obesity epidemic was directly related to the number of parks in America that were shutting down. In the third story, he tied it all together by explaining how lawyers sit in parks and wait for kids to fall so that they can sue the city.

Looking back, I realize that George Will had a masterful way of blending emotion and logic. He was this conservative-looking guy dressed in a suit, with nerdy glasses, who could cite facts with the best of them. He wasn't brash like Bill O'Reilly or funny like Jon Stewart, but believe me, you could feel his emotion. He knew how to tug at your heartstrings. For one hour, he told stories about all the problems in America, and I can honestly say that I have never been more inspired! Suddenly, I felt as though the world was looking for somebody to go out there and help solve these problems. I had this notion that God himself was calling on me to be one of these people.

When the event ended, my friend Bill introduced me to George and said, "What could you tell Patrick? He's thirty years old. He's done very well in sales at a young age. But he feels he needs a mission to take his life to the next level."

George said, "Where are you from, and what's your background like?"

When I told him I was from Iran, he asked me more about my family. I told him that my mom's family was communist and my dad was an imperialist. I shared how we escaped from Iran in 1989 during the war, lived in a refugee camp in Germany for two years, and then moved to California when I was twelve.

George was a great listener and had that gift of making me feel like he really cared. He said, "Why don't you go study why America has the most immigrants out of all the countries in the world? Why don't you go study capitalism and see why it's the greatest system? What people around the world want more than anything is freedom. Go find out why so many people hate capitalism so you can see the other side." He also told me to find out why there's only one country in the world whose name is identified with the word "dream." There's no Russian Dream or Chinese Dream. There's only the American dream.

I took that advice to heart. I thanked him for his time, and as soon as I left, I started studying. I say all the time that you can **predict success by how quickly people move at the speed of instruction**. Whether it's feedback from a mentor or a book recommendation from a friend, watch how quickly people act on this advice, and you'll learn a lot. After speaking with George Will, I read everything I could about immigration, capitalism, and political science. I didn't need motivation to study. I couldn't think about much else besides the American dream and the history behind it.

The next day, we had our 10:00 a.m. Saturday sales meeting. I loved these Saturday meetings. Coming up with new messages to inspire people was one of the highlights of my week. But for the past few months, something was different. Looking back, I can see that I was in the process of discovering my real mission and re-creating myself.

This meeting was different. George Will's speech had ignited my mission. I gave a nineteen-minute speech about the future of America. I had never talked like a patriot before, and my intensity level was off the charts. Many people at the meeting were first-generation Americans. I challenged them in a tone that surprised even me as I asked, "Why did your parents come to this country?"

I had never felt so alive.

Everybody was looking at me funny, saying how much my message had changed. I normally would only talk about dreams. But this speech was different. Everything was about keeping freedom in America. Why did so many people leave Iran? Why did so many people leave Russia? Why does every other country in the world talk about the American dream? I was lit up. I had connected to my mission, and from that point on, I've been on fire. I went from being a guy who had made a million dollars but had no direction to being a man on a mission.

My mission was, and still is, to use entrepreneurship to solve the world's problems and teach capitalism *because* the fate of the world depends on it.

A few months after George Will's speech, I realized I couldn't live out my mission as a sales leader. I needed real influence. My first move was to present my vision to the large financial services firm that I was affiliated with. It was not received well. They wanted me to be the guy who put up big numbers and talked about results, not ideas. Keeping my mouth shut and cashing checks was never going to fulfill me. That's when I knew I had to risk it all to do it the way I wanted to do it. I needed to do more. I needed to become an entrepreneur.

When I started my financial services firm, our mission statement was to bring back the free enterprise system and hope to American families. To this day, I'm convinced that the more people I can show how to make their own money through business, the more problems we will solve and the freer we will be.

We'll return to dreams and the dream language I had relied on so much before in the next chapter. Dreams still matter. But it's by design that the mission has to come before the dream. Had I not discovered mine, I'd have all the trappings of a dream life, but I would have felt empty. After George Will's speech, everything completely changed. I had a mission to correct an injustice.

Did you also notice how my mission incorporated what I love (freedom, hope, capitalism), what I hate (restrictions, despair, communism), and what bothers me (manipulation, lack of choices)? If you haven't already, it's time to begin answering those questions yourself.

REPLACE *JUST* WITH *BECAUSE*

Some of you may have read these stories and started writing down your mission. Others of you may be thinking hard about how to define your mission. Then there's some of you who are ready to defend why you don't need one. I've sat with many people who have fought for their reasons not to have a mission. When they spell out what they want to do with their lives, all their statements have one word in common: "just."

1. I just want to make a decent living and not have to worry about money.
2. I just want to make enough money so I can travel the world.

3. I just want a simple life where I can serve my church and live in peace.
4. I just want to be able to meet payroll, fund my retirement, and be home for dinner by six.
5. I just want to build a business that my kids can eventually run.

You may think that I'm judging these people for thinking too small. You would be wrong. My issue is that they are the ones diminishing their own mission. By using the word "just," they are either limiting themselves or haven't taken the time to "recruit" their mission.

You have to ask yourself why you are using the word "just." Is it because you are afraid to fail? Or are you being realistic because you're honest about how much work you are willing to put in? Or is it because you haven't done enough reflection to discover your true mission?

Even if you don't want to go beneath the surface, there is a simple tool that will help you refine your mission. Simply remove the word "just." Let's look at two examples:

1. I just want to make enough money so I can travel the world.
2. I just want a simple life where I can serve my church and live in peace.

Now remove the word "just."

1. I want to make enough money so I can travel the world.
2. I want a simple life where I can serve my church and live in peace.

You have already created a stronger statement. The next leap is to make the decision to transition from "I want to . . ." to "I'm on a mission to . . ."

1. I'm on a mission to make enough money so I can travel the world.
2. I'm on a mission to live a simple life where I can serve my church and live in peace.

You may be asking, "Pat, is that a good enough mission?" Only you can answer that question. Say it out loud and see what emotion it stirs up. Say it while looking in the mirror and see what happens to your body language. If it feels good, it probably works. Say it to others and see how you feel. If you're self-conscious, that's telling you something. If you feel a sense of pride, that's also valuable information. These are just a few litmus tests. If you don't feel like your mission is working, keep refining it.

Another powerful tool is to add the word "because" at the end and fill in the rest of the sentence. Ellen Langer, a Harvard psychologist, conducted experiments on how effective the word "because" is. The key point is that no matter what you say after the word "because," the mission becomes more powerful.

1. I'm on a mission to make enough money so I can travel the world *because* you only live once and I'm lucky enough to do what my parents couldn't.
2. I'm on a mission to live a simple life where I can serve my church and live in peace *because* I'm dedicated to my faith and know that simplicity brings me closer to what matters in life.

Let's put it all together and revisit the final mission statement example above: I just want to build a business that my kids can eventually run.

I get the feeling that this person is afraid to declare what he actually wants—and the choice of words weakens his mission. Take out the word "just," add "because," and sharpen the words, and it will change to a more honest and more powerful statement.

I want to build a business that makes a difference and creates generational wealth because I have what it takes and I love my family.

Do you see what just happened? Even though the content of the mission didn't change that much, the impact was substantial. That's a lot different from minimizing it by using the word "just."

Your mission may or may not change much by the end of this chapter, or even by the end of this month. But if all you do is eliminate the word "just," add the word "because," and take the time to see how it feels, you are well on your way.

SWOT ANALYSIS

Getting emotional? Can you feel the blood coursing through your veins? Great. I want you to keep building the muscle of shifting from emotion to logic, because we're going to get more logical to build the plan block.

Before you start making any plan, though, you have to orient yourself. When you see a map, the first thing you look for are the words "You are here." You can't start making plans before you know where you stand now.

SWOT stands for strengths, weaknesses, opportunities, and threats. Depending on where you are in your career, you've either done SWOT analyses dozens of times or this will be the first. Either way, what makes this different is that you are bringing two things to the exercise this time that may not have existed before: *emotion* and *radical honesty*. The questions that led you to reflect on your mission likely brought out both confidence and painful truths.

You may have said something like "I've always wanted to retire my parents, but I've never been organized enough to reach a six-figure income." With that statement, your weakness is staring right at you.

Maybe you said, "I'm going to make health care more efficient because the solution has yet to be found, and I know I can do it." There's your opportunity. You may also see in that statement that there will be threats from public policy and better-capitalized competitors. Or you'll note that your lack of knowledge in technology and analytics may hold you back.

The work you do on your mission feeds directly into your plan. Whatever came out of the previous exercises should lead you to plug the information into your SWOT analysis. I recommend you do this for yourself and for your business, knowing there will be some crossover. For your business, you can do this with a team. For now, focus on the personal so you can start to build your own plan for the year.

Strengths	Weaknesses
Work ethic	Leadership
Coachability	The ability to manage multiple projects
Industry knowledge	
Laser-sharp focus	Disorganization
	Listening

Opportunities	Threats
Scaling the business	Poor health/low energy
Opening new markets	Losing employees to competitors
Being more productive	Running short on capital
Developing new leaders	Interest rates/market conditions

I created that list to give you some ideas, but of course your list is going to be specific to you. If you haven't already integrated your SWOT analysis into your skill-building, it's worth revisiting. If, for example, you feel like you're not a good listener and that may cause some of your top performers to leave you, you know what skill you need to work on.

Let's explore all four quadrants in more detail.

Strengths

For strengths, leverage what you do best.

Looking at your strengths is a great way to identify your opportunities. If you're a great closer or a great sales trainer, but you're too busy with the day-to-day chores of running the business to do these activities, there's an opportunity! The best solution is to calendar those activities into your week. Maybe you get back to running the sales meeting or at least run a monthly training. Another idea is to let your team know that for big accounts, you want to be in those pitch meetings.

If you're a brilliant researcher who keeps getting pulled into writing grants, you have to find a way to get back into the lab. Elon Musk is an engineer at heart who loves to experiment and collaborate with other great thinkers. Even though he gets pulled away for things like compliance and investor relations, for both his sanity and his soul, he needs to find time to tinker. Bottom line: If you're not utilizing your strengths, if you're not doing what created success in the first place, you risk losing that success.

Weaknesses

For weaknesses, build skills, delegate, or mitigate.

I realized early on in my career that I wasn't the most organized person. I actually think that being disorganized ties into my strength of being creative. My solution is, rather than fixing this weakness, I set up systems so that it doesn't slow me down. That means I delegate and make sure I have organized people in my inner circle. I hired a personal assistant before I was making six figures because I knew I would never make six figures without one. In my personal life, I trust my wife to handle the kids' activities and our social calendar. She tells me when to show up and that works for me.

Most people are very aware of their strengths but have blind spots about their weaknesses. There's something tricky about weaknesses. That's why I often refer to them as *leaks*. The things you hide from others are also the things you're afraid to acknowledge or write down. You go to the casino too often, but nobody knows about it. You could be addicted to social media, spend hours on your fantasy football team, stop at the McDonald's drive-through on your way home from work, or flirt to get attention. Those are all weaknesses that many of us don't want to admit. They drain our energy, wallet, and time. If not addressed, these leaks can turn into downpours that destroy your bottom line and your well-being.

Opportunities

For opportunities, keep asking what's possible, don't worry about the "how."

Opportunities are exciting. This is where you ask a lot of "what if" questions.

- What if we can raise our price by 15 percent without losing any market share?
- What if we can find a sales leader who can make our existing team better and free me up to work on leadership development?
- What if we can hire a personal assistant for a few of our executives—how much more productive will they be?

- What if we can add a new product to our mix?
- What if we can hire a producer who is so talented that our page views triple?

Threats

For threats, cultivate a paranoia mindset.

What are your threats for the upcoming year and for the next decade? You've brought family into the business. What happens if they start arguing? Like with weaknesses, either you deal with threats directly or you delegate. Do you need to research every topic? Is it better to do it yourself or is it worth paying someone else to do that research? For example, if you're a hedge fund investing in emerging markets, there will always be geopolitical threats. You likely don't have the time or resources to stay on top of them, so you contract that out.

If poor health, burnout, or low energy are threats, you build that into your plan. It might mean hiring a personal trainer or it could be installing a gym at your office and hiring someone to teach yoga twice a week. In that case, you are mitigating both a personal threat and a threat to your organization.

Notice how emotion and logic are tied into the SWOT analysis. If a threat is losing people, the logical thing is to sit down with your HR team (if you don't have one, sub it out/hire a consultant) to work on your compensation plan and your employment contracts. At the same time, figure out how to show people you care so that you create loyalty. If that's a weakness (and it is for many leaders), add "show people that I care" to the weakness column and build that into your plan.

Are you seeing how this is an integrated plan? And are you seeing that you can't work on the *plan* without working on the *person?* That person, of course, is the only person you're going to spend every minute of the rest of your life with. YOU!

GET AHEAD OF THE TOPICS TO WATCH

Let's get a bit more specific with the details of your plan. You need to have a list of the most newsworthy topics to follow closely each year in order to plan around them. In some years, it will be elections. In other years, it will be changes to the tax code. These topics and these dates will shape your strategy and your calendar. Plus, by seeing the big picture of the world around you, you start to work more ON the business and less IN the business.

This may seem obvious, but even at business conferences, I'm surprised at the number of hands that don't go up when I ask who reads *The Wall Street Journal.* We all need to be reading it. Even if you're in a specialized industry, you need to be aware of business and geopolitical news.

Talking about COVID-19 will make us all sound like dinosaurs, though heading into 2021, it was at the top of everyone's list. You needed a plan to deal with mandates and adapt to working from home. As the narrative and unemployment shift, you have to keep updating your plan to meet the needs of your employees and customers. You can't do this without knowing what's happening around you. And while topics like the supply chain will always be relevant, you need to be much more specific. If, for example, you're in the transportation business, you have to look at railroad strikes, pipeline legislation, and tax incentives for clean energy. If you're in the financial industry, you have to constantly monitor inflation, unemployment, interest rates, and new regulations.

There are enough surprises that you'll never be able to see in advance. That's why you need to be way ahead of events that you know will be happening. Don't say you can't predict a labor strike—or at least the possibility of one. You know the dates when collective bargaining agreements expire. You know when key employment contracts end. You know what federal, state, and local elections are happening before the year starts.

Just as there are topics to pay attention to, there are certain people you should be paying attention to as well. Maybe you know there's a big executive at a rival company who is rumored to be retiring. You want to watch him or her because it creates both threats and opportunities. A change in leadership means people will be free agents and looking to leave the company. Or maybe the company hires a more aggressive CEO to recruit *your* people. You need to plan for all of these possibilities.

To give you some guidance on creating your topics and people lists, here are things to consider:

1. Industry
2. Politics
3. Economy/inflation
4. Regulation
5. Key dates for labor contracts
6. Leaders in transition

OPERATIONS PLAN: CALENDAR THE ENTIRE YEAR

You're going to have a board meeting on the day of your kid's recital. Your company retreat is going to fall on the same day as your cousin's graduation. This is inevitable. When the late Kobe Bryant played for the Lakers, they almost always had a game on Christmas Day. When I interviewed him, he said he dealt with this by planning out his entire year in advance in order to avoid surprises. Instead of winging it, you get ahead of it.

If you know you're going to miss an important event, you schedule time with that person for another day. If you can't see them, you show them extra love and invest in a special gift or gesture. Your calendar has to go twelve months out. For every month, map out every single campaign, retreat, strategy session, board meeting, and quarterly review.

Most people have holidays pop up in their calendars. You can start there, as they'll often be reminders. Learn from your mistakes. If you constantly fight with your spouse about your lame approach to Valentine's Day, put it on your calendar for January 14, one month ahead. All you need is to make a note in your calendar to start shopping for a gift or planning an outing.

When we discuss the systems building block in the next chapter, I'll show you a few more strategies for how to leverage your calendar. For now, I'll tell you that I'm always at least one quarter ahead in my planning. If your sales typically slump in the summer, set up an off-site strategy session on March 1 so you're ten weeks ahead of it. Go back to your SWOT analysis and your skill set and start to fill in your calendar. Find three conferences and schedule them now. When you sign up and pay the deposit, you've taken an important step toward addressing a weakness.

PLAN FOR THE CRISIS BEFORE IT HAPPENS

In my last book, *Your Next Five Moves*, we looked closely at grandmasters in chess and how they see fifteen moves ahead. When creating your business plan, you need to anticipate and make the shift from being reactive to being proactive. You do so by making contingency plans long before a crisis happens.

Seth Godin, author of numerous bestsellers including *Tribes* and *The Song of Significance*, said, "The most exciting thing about professional project management is that it trades away excitement for systems thinking and intentional action. We make heroes out of people who show up with the last-minute save, but the real work is in not needing the last minute."

If you live in New Orleans, the Philippines, or Florida, and you're not thinking about hurricanes or typhoons, you're being naive. You need a plan in place before they hit. To do so, study history. What patterns do they follow? What do you need to do well in advance?

Our financial services company's headquarters are in Dallas, Texas. We've experienced multiple tornadoes and even winter freezes. Pipes blowing up, power outages, and slick roads led to schools shutting down—and our IT systems as well. All of these events required us to anticipate the worst-case scenario and be prepared for it. Whether it was buying laptops or hotspots, we always had a contingency plan in case the internet didn't work at our office or employees' homes.

When a crisis does hit, whether it's a natural disaster or only related to your business, what extends or decreases the lifespan of a crisis? Your planning or, in some cases, lack of planning.

There is nothing you can do to prevent a crisis from happening. You can, however, minimize the impact of it based on how you react to it. Dwight D. Eisenhower said, "In preparing for battle I have always found that plans are useless, but planning is indispensable." Ike wasn't quite as creative as the British Army, which invented an adage called the 7 Ps: *Proper Planning and Preparation Prevents Piss Poor Performance.*

Having a plan in place creates poise as a leader. We all have the potential to come unglued. The ones who remain calm are the ones who have already played out the scenario in advance. When a crisis happens, some overreact and some underreact. Think about crises on a scale from one to ten. A nine increases your urgency. You turn a nine into a two and you're in trouble.

Your ability to see five to fifteen moves ahead allows you to *anticipate* a crisis. When it's already been addressed in your business, it allows you to handle it with precision. I put plans in place for all scenarios, both good and bad, to happen. Some say I'm being negative or pessimistic. I call it logical crisis planning because when the crisis comes, I don't want to be all those negative words that often get labeled as emotion. When things go down, the last thing I want is to be impulsive, irrational, melodramatic, temperamental, or hot-blooded.

I want to have already thought through my moves. I do everything I can to prevent bad things from happening, *and* I also map out my first three to five moves if something bad does happen.

There's a reason I use the metaphor of chess in business. It's also why I study the Mafia so much. Expert planning means seeing things before they happen. Maybe somebody on the inside's trying to make a power play. You have to see that before it takes hold. Maybe you need to strengthen relationships with your key players. Maybe you need to get a little closer. If your team members are intimidated by you, they're going to withhold information. They'll hide bad news from you to avoid feeling your wrath. That creates a lot of risk to the sustainability of your business. Start interacting with your team more and get to know them better. Show them that you care to build loyalty. If you really want to build depth, ask them who their enemies are!

Threats are always lurking. If you're constantly in your office with the door closed, you're going to miss a lot. Walk around and circulate among the troops. If most of your work is virtual, call and text more. Make unannounced office visits. Keep an eye out for signs of unrest.

Then start to play the "if" game.

If I lose my biggest customer, what happens?

When I ask that question, I start working on how I can prevent that from happening. Maybe I've taken that customer for granted. It's a common but reckless mistake to put all your energy into customer acquisition and neglect your current customers. You fall into the bad habit of letting everybody else on your team deal with your customers. Maybe you have to pick up the phone more, schedule an in-person meeting, or send a gift.

Do you see the pattern? Identify the threat or potential crisis. Then create a plan to address it before it happens. Keep asking yourself questions like, If I lose my biggest sales rep or biggest revenue producer, what happens?

That question takes you down a similar path. What do you need to do to prevent a superstar from leaving you? How's your relationship with her, on a scale from zero to ten? Let's say you rate it a five. Well, maybe you've got to take her out to an event and spend some time with her and her family to show her how much you care about her. She needs to know that. That's part of your plan. Here are some other "what ifs" to consider:

1. If my current office doesn't work out and I'm forced to relocate, what happens?
2. What if we run short on cash?
3. If I go on disability for three months, what's the replacement plan?
4. What's the impact of labor or material costs rising?
5. What if we get sued?
6. If we have to scale up quickly to hire more staff, how do we speed up the process? Are we better off adding to our HR team or hiring a recruiting firm?

An even better way to ask questions is to build in solutions to the question. When you frame a question this way, you move directly to action. For example: If my staff tries to unionize or goes on strike, what are my first three moves? See how you created a better question?

When you frame the question by asking what your next three to five moves are, it gets you moving to create concrete plans. Consider question five, "What if we get sued?" Do you see how this question doesn't put you in solution mode? It's better to ask, "If we get sued, what are our first three moves?" If move one is *finding* an attorney and you don't have one, you've exposed a weakness. You need to act *now* so you have legal counsel standing by.

Open-ended questions are only a little better. A fair answer to "If we run short on cash, what happens?" might be "We panic." Or you might say, "We'll set up a line of credit." By then, it's too late. Wouldn't it be better if you had planned three moves ahead for running short on cash?

Those moves might be to

1. tap into an *existing* line of credit;
2. suspend all unnecessary travel and all but urgent new hires;
3. reengage with Susan, who had inquired about an equity stake in the company.

These are the types of questions you need to be asking and answering. I ask them of my team all the time. When I ask a "what if" question and a person says, "I don't know," do you know what I say?

"I know exactly what will happen. You are going to freak out because you don't have a plan. If you haven't thought about it *before* it happens, you've set yourself up for failure."

The simple step of planning for a crisis and mapping out at least three moves is a critical part of your business plan.

KEEP YOUR MISSION CURRENT

I mentioned that shortly after hearing George Will's speech, I started my own firm in 2009. In 2022, I sold that firm for multi-nine figures. On the day the deal closed, did anything change about my mission? Did I stop making content? Did I shut down Valuetainment? Did I stop working on Saturdays?

If I have more money than I need to live, why am I not slowing down?

My mission was never about becoming rich. Money was simply a by-product of my mission, which means it will never be complete. There will always be problems to solve, entrepreneurs who need guidance, and threats to capitalism.

That being said, the specifics of your mission may change. For me, the big picture stays constant. My mission will always be to elevate, empower, and influence. I want to be a kingmaker, meaning that when I pour my leadership into someone, they reach new heights.

One way to keep your mission current is with your language. Even as things change, be vigilant about being a person who says "I just want to" versus one who says "I'm on a mission to" person.

USE YOUR MISSION TO BUILD YOUR PLAN

After I heard George Will's speech, I told myself, "There's no way in the world that I'm here to do something small." Neither are you. Nobody who has read or listened this far was put here to do something small with their life. As you learned in this building block, you have to put in the time to recruit your mission. Some of that is downtime. Remember that the "work" is allowing your mission to come through. Once it does, the logical part of your plan will follow effortlessly.

The biggest thing I want you to remember for planning is to anticipate. Always be at least three to five moves ahead. Very little should catch you off guard. When a crisis does occur, the cautious majority will panic. When you're part of the audacious few, you are already in solution mode, taking steps that have been well rehearsed.

YOUR BLOCKS

MISSION

Action:

1. How will you recruit your mission? What questions must you ask to find the fire inside of you?

2. What cause are you fighting for? What injustice are you correcting? What crusade are you leading?

3. What are the things you love? What are the things you hate that you would finally feel brave enough to fight against? What are the things that bother you that you would want to change?

4. Write out a mission without the word "just" and with the word "because."

5. Do at least two litmus tests to see how it feels:
   a. Say it out loud.
   b. Say it in front of the mirror and watch your body language.
   c. Say it to others and make note of how you feel.

6. Be honest about getting complacent. If you feel bored, have plateaued, or are distracted by toys, it's a sign to revisit your mission.

PLAN

Action:

1. Complete a SWOT analysis. Be honest about your weaknesses/leaks and get excited asking "what if" questions.

2. Based on the SWOT analysis, plan out improvements for three areas in your business.

3. List the three to five moves you would make if you suddenly had to go on disability or sick leave, or if a disaster occurred and you were no longer there to run your company.

4. Ask "if" questions for at least seven scenarios and make sure you map out at least your first three to five moves.

CHAPTER 7

Dreams and Systems

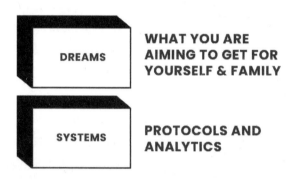

Bad habits repeat themselves again and again not because you don't want to change, but because you have the wrong system for change. You do not rise to the level of your goals. You fall to the level of your systems.

James Clear, *Atomic Habits*

fell in love with baseball at age thirteen. I had barely been in America for a year, and it became my obsession. I didn't like books back then, but I loved the *Daily News* because the sports section had the most statistics. Baseball captured my attention, because there was more data to analyze than in the other sports. When I got lost in the numbers of batting averages and on-base percentages, my mind would wander. I had no talent for the game, and I was never on an organized team, but I still had a dream of one day playing in the major leagues.

A lot of kids get to play out their fantasies on Little League fields. I buried my nose in the magazine *Beckett*, which listed the price of every baseball card. Each month, I would get a new issue and look up the value of the cards of my favorite players: Joe DiMaggio, Lou Gehrig, Yogi Berra, Babe Ruth, and Mickey Mantle. I thought to myself: What if one day I could own a Babe Ruth rookie card? That was second on my list behind a 1952 Mickey Mantle Topps card. Back then, it was valued at $33,000. In 2023, there are only three 1952 Mickey Mantle Topps cards graded PSA 10, and they are worth between $20 and $30 million. At least I don't have to kick myself for not buying it, since I didn't exactly have thirty-three grand sitting in my savings account back then.

These cards were the gateway to my dreams. I remember, in eighth grade, walking home on Verdugo Road in Glendale with my friends from Wilson Junior High School. I would ask, "Can you imagine if, one day, you could own a major league baseball team? Which team would it be?" Most said our hometown Dodgers, and one of my buddies, who loved Ted Williams, said the Boston Red Sox. Because of the cards, my answer was always the Yankees. The New York Yankees.

It was a crazy dream. It made no sense. If I had said that I actually believed this dream would ever come true, I would have been committed to an insane asylum. But every great achievement starts with a thought, and every audacious goal begins with a dream.

In this chapter, I invite you to dream big. I challenge you to come up with ideas that will make people question your sanity. It's only by thinking this way that the impossible can happen. I'm talking about something as crazy as my becoming an owner of not just any major league franchise but the one in the Bronx that has won twenty-seven World Series titles.

When I got the call with the opportunity to be a minority owner of the New York Yankees, it took me back to Verdugo Road and my childhood dream.

I had been looking at other ownership opportunities in sports, but when the Yankees called, I immediately told my lawyer to start the process. Between Major League Baseball and the Yankees, there were thirteen months of background checks and interviews. Just when it seemed like there weren't any more tests to pass, the last step was to fly to the Bronx for one of the most important meetings of my life. I sat in a room with four members of the top Yankee brass: Hal Steinbrenner, managing general partner and cochairperson; Randy Levine, president; Lonn A. Trost, chief operating officer; and Tony Bruno, chief financial officer of Yankee Global Enterprises. It turned out that the interview was the easiest part. They were my kind of guys—open, respectful, and not afraid of the truth.

Finally, in June 2023, when I was in Bermuda, my lawyer called and said, "Congratulations, you're officially an owner of the New York Yankees." My 1.8 GPA and I now get to sit in the owner's box and get the best seat in the house to see all the retired jerseys, all the championship banners, and all the ghosts of the players whose cards I used to dream about. Sure, it's been fun to acquire many of the cards—and I still dream about that 1952 Topps Mickey Mantle. But to become a minority owner of the New York Yankees still beats them all. It reminds me that no dream is too big and to keep dreaming.

If you want to be a part of the audacious few, you must start with audacious dreams.

Most people bother to dream only once per year. Every new year offers a fresh start and a chance to make resolutions. So why is it that New Year's resolutions have a 92 percent failure rate? And why is it that, despite that failure rate, almost half of American adults make at least one resolution every year? As we talked about earlier, 50 percent of businesses fail within five years and 70 percent fail within ten years. So why do people keep writing ineffective business plans?

It's because they still have dreams and have the ability to tap into emotion, but they're usually missing the logical *systems*.

We already know that emotion is critical to a successful business plan. As a leader, as I mentioned in the last chapter, I'm constantly speaking the "dream language." I share stories about my four kids. I talk about the arguments I have with my wife. I tear up when I talk about my dad. I also talk about how broke I was and how ashamed I felt when I couldn't afford to pay my dad's medical bills or had $49,000 in credit card debt.

It's not as depressing as it sounds!

Mixed in with my struggles are reminders of what I said at my lowest points, what kept me motivated, and how I've always used my haters as fuel. But I also know how to tie these stories back to the systems that keep the company running. My business meetings are equal parts dream casting and analytics-driven strategy sessions. We tie our dreams to logical systems so that there are clear actions to take to build our envisioned future.

WHAT YOU WILL LEARN IN THIS CHAPTER

I think of systems as *dream-making machines*. You could also call systems *hero-making machines*. The dream may be to win the Mr. Olympia competition. The systems are the workouts, nutrition, supplements, recovery, and stretching. Equally important is the sequencing of these systems and the commitment to refining and reinforcing each step.

7 Steps to Create a Dream-Making Machine

1. Speak the dream language at least 20 percent of the time.
2. Turn your dreams into specific goals.
3. Make your goals visual.
4. Create the systems to make your dreams and goals a reality.
5. Analyze data and trends to improve the systems.
6. Keep refining existing systems and look to create new ones.
7. Remember to always speak the dream language—and make it emotional!

Dreams spark the fire and make you (or your team) want to achieve, but without systems to accomplish tasks, you won't be able to channel that emotion to drive success. Plus, if every time you take action to accomplish your dream, you have to create a new system, inefficiency will kill you. That's why it's so important to create systems that are duplicatable.

In this chapter, you will learn how to speak the dream language to others. In fact, as a rule, I tell my executive team that everything they say has to be at least 20 percent dream language. You can't ask people to execute before getting them to "see" where it's going and tapping into what their hearts desire.

If the dream excites you, you'll work as much as you need. Thinking about what you want is the dream. The emotion comes from picturing what your life will look like when you achieve your goals. If the plan is clear, you and your team will know how to create systems to direct your energy and accomplish tasks.

LEARN THE DREAM LANGUAGE: IMAGINE IF ONE DAY

Since most people are short-term thinkers who struggle to delay gratification, it's up to the leader to describe how a person's life will look a year from now, a decade from now, and fifty years from now, depending on the effort they put in today. Use your talent and passion as a dream caster to show people what their life will look like when they take the disciplined path. Do the same for yourself.

Most people are so caught up in the here and now that they don't even try to see the future. A great prompt is "Imagine if one day . . ." That's how my dream to own part of the Yankees started.

Take a moment now to fill in what comes next. Allow yourself to dream: "Imagine if one day I . . ."

- Win the Nobel Prize
- Launch a billion-dollar IPO
- Discover a cure for cancer
- Revolutionize secondary-school education
- Love what I do so much that it doesn't feel like work

Another simple prompt for the dream language is "It would be incredible to . . ."

- Live in a house with a view of the ocean
- Send my kids to the best private school
- Look at my bank balance and see another zero
- Never have to look at the prices on a menu or travel site

Here are a few other prompts to tap into your dreams:

1. What would my life look life if . . .
2. What I'm aiming to get for myself and my family is . . .
3. What I most look forward to is . . .
4. My bucket list includes . . .

I can only get you started. Remember that the reason to think about your dreams is to create emotion. Keep using these prompts until you get to a place where these dreams excite you.

GOALS ARE DREAMS WITH DEADLINES AND REWARDS

I had a sales rep who made $36,000 in one year. He wrote a killer business plan, worked tirelessly on his skill gaps, and created efficient systems. The following year, things started to click, and he made $72,000 in one *month*. When I asked him how he celebrated, he looked totally confused.

I asked, "Did you take your wife to a luxury hotel for a staycation? Did you at least go to a high-end restaurant? Did you buy a new suit?"

I heard nothing but crickets.

He didn't do one thing to celebrate. The next month, his income went from $72,000 to $5,400. Because he hadn't rewarded himself the previous month, his subconscious was wondering, *Why am I busting my tail for nothing?* By sitting in the bank, that money didn't create any emotion. His problem was that he hadn't experienced the emotions from the reward that would drill into his subconscious the value of hard work.

Most people are very good at rewarding themselves when they make money, and more often than not, they overdo it. But every once in a while, it's the complete opposite. Both you and your family have to see the reward of your working as hard as you are, or else what's the point? Why would you keep putting in the effort?

Thinking about how you will celebrate makes your dreams come alive.

The emotion generated by this building block comes from picturing what your life will look like when you achieve your dreams.

What's the "I" word that's so important in capitalism?

Incentive.

What if you whoop some ass this year? What are you going to do?

Your psyche has to be rewarded for paying a price. You program your psyche by using a reward to reinforce your dream. When you decide on the award *in advance* of achieving your dream, you are programming your mind to believe *I'm willing to pay a price because this reward is going to happen.* This is a continuous feedback loop that you must integrate into your plan.

Before we return to rewards, let's talk about goals. Goals are the specific outcomes we aim for on our way to achieving our dreams. Dreams direct our energy; goals take that direction and create a laser focus. When goals are specific and measurable, giving us deadlines and putting rewards in place, they work.

Effective Goals

- Specific
- Measurable
- Have a deadline
- Rewards in place
  - When I do X, I will treat myself to Y.
  - When I do X, I will treat my friends and family to Y.

A POWERFUL DREAM BECOMES
A FUTURE TRUTH

Walt Disney was on a mission to make people happy. That made him excited to get out of bed every morning. But it *didn't* direct his actions. He needed to take the next step by declaring specific dreams. Turning his mission into dreams would look this:

- My dream is to have a theme park that's the happiest place on earth.
- My dream is to create movies that make people happy.
- My dream is to have an Experimental Prototype Community of Tomorrow (EPCOT) that creates a happy and healthy community.

We have a tendency to use the words "dreams" and "goals" interchangeably. Notice that I listed Walt Disney's dreams and not his goals. If they were goals, they would be specific and have a deadline. Both have their place. There's benefit in dreaming without knowing exactly when and how you will get there. There are other times when you want to be crystal clear on the action plan and time frame.

Whether you are talking about dreams or goals, they must make you emotional. They also have to find that delicate balance of being a stretch and being attainable. Having five hundred thousand licensed agents by 2029 seemed like a stretch, but for me, anything less would not have fired me up. It would have felt like settling, a concession to mediocrity. I agree with Richard Branson's quote that "if your dreams don't scare you, they are too small."

Jay-Z said, "I believe you can speak things into existence." Some may say that's impossible. Others go to the other extreme and believe that words alone can make a difference. They think if they pray long enough or keep making positive affirmations, results will follow. What I've learned is that without the belief *and* the systems to go along with those dreams, it won't be enough.

It's like that expression "Trust in God, but lock your car." You need to do your part. When you are talking a big game and putting in the effort to get there, you become that powerful person on a mission and your success reinforces itself. You get to a point where your dreams become your *future truth*.

My definition of future truth is to live in the present as if what you're aiming for has already become a reality. I express my dreams with the conviction that they are going to happen.

I've seen time and time again how that conviction is contagious. If you don't 100 percent believe it, no one will.

If you really are working with the focus, urgency, and conviction of someone living their future truth, you will be inspired. This will create a chain reaction in which other people will get inspired by you. It's the reason we're enamored with visionaries. If everything you do is consistent with a person who is on a mission and committed to his or her dreams, you will get others to follow you.

MAKE YOUR DREAMS AND GOALS VISUAL

Take the time now to figure out how you will make your dreams visual, so they are staring you in the face every day. Put your dreams in front of you. Make vision boards. See how your mission feeds into your dreams. For example, I made vision boards relating to lifestyle (the things I wanted), market domination (I don't want to just compete—that's how I'm wired!), and people who have made history (they move me—and I dream of joining them).

How will you create visuals that are constantly connecting you to your dreams? Because I was once a Hummer mechanic, I had a dream of one day buying a yellow Hummer. I gave myself the goal of increasing my savings to $1 million in twelve months. If I hit this goal, I told myself, only then could I begin the process of buying the yellow Hummer.

My first step? I put a picture of a yellow Hummer in twenty different places. I couldn't even see the speedometer on my car because there was a picture of a yellow Hummer there! On my phone, a yellow Hummer. On my mirror, a yellow Hummer. When I would open up my wallet, a yellow Hummer.

I used every visual I could think of to imprint this yellow Hummer in my conscious and subconscious mind. And guess what? A year later, I got the yellow Hummer. It has to be in front of your face all the time.

I encourage you to get creative. It may help to have a friend who is good at Photoshop . . . or add that to your skill list! If your dream, for example, is to retire your parents, on the screen saver for your phone or computer, put a picture of them with big smiles sitting on the porch of the house you're going to buy them.

There is a Jewish tradition in which a mezuzah, a parchment with religious text, is placed on the doorframe of a home. What's written on the parchment comes from this passage in Deuteronomy 6:9: "And you shall inscribe them upon the doorposts of your house and upon your gates, in order that your days and the days of your children shall increase, on the land which the Lord swore to your forefathers to give to them, as the days of heaven above the earth."

After the mezuzah is placed on the doorframe, every time a Jewish person enters their home, they have a visual reminder of their dreams. What symbol or visual will you use to keep your dreams constantly in front of you?

Like all strategies, there is risk when you don't execute well. Don't put up a bunch of motivational posters in your office that don't mean anything. If you hang a bunch of generic signs with goals that you are not actively driving, you become a cliché. The better move is to make your own signs that fit your dreams and build traditions around them.

At the University of Notre Dame, there's a sign in the tunnel between the locker room and the football field that says, "Play Like a Champion Today." As the football players pass the sign on their way to the field, it's a visual cue to uphold the university's tradition and give their all each game.

In the conference room at Valuetainment, we had an artist paint the following quotation from William Goldman: "Nobody knows anything . . . Not one person in the entire motion picture field knows for a certainty what's going to work. Every time out it's a guess and, if you're lucky, an educated one."

We did this because we want to make visual our dream of being a company that encourages creativity and risk-taking. We want the idea that every creative endeavor requires risk *inscribed* on our walls, so it becomes inscribed in our subconscious minds.

Here are some other places for visuals:

- Bathroom mirror
- Photos in your wallet
- Vision boards placed in strategic locations
- Phone and computer screen savers
- Art you create for your home and/or office

SYSTEMS MAKE THE DREAM WORK

Up until now, we have focused on the dream building block. It's time to turn our attention to the systems that allow you to accomplish your goals. For example, let's say your goal is to add another zero to your bank account in a set period of time. Whether you're aiming to go from $10,000 to $100,000, $1 million to $10 million, or $100 million to $1 billion, the system will be the same. For this example, let's say you want to go from $10,000 to $100,000 in three years. That's ninety grand in thirty-six months, which means you need to put away $2,500 per month.

One of the best systems for saving money is to *pay your savings first.* Most people do the opposite. They see what's left at the end of the month and then save it. That is a system, albeit a lousy one. When you pay your savings first, you hit your goal right away and often don't even miss the money. Just as you automatically pay your rent, car insurance, and cell phone bill, the savings becomes a fixed, automatic cost.

Let's say you're early in your business career and can only do $1,500 per month. Now you need to either make $12,000 a year more or spend $12,000 less. Maybe you pick a side hustle as a bartender or Uber driver where you can earn $500 per weekend. Do it twice a month and you're there. If that starts getting old, you build up the wins and confidence to ask for a raise. Maybe that gets you $700 per month, and you can cut out a few happy hours to save $300. At that point, start paying your savings $2,500 first. It won't take but one or two times for you to run short of money at the end of month to alter your spending. Plus, it may not even bother you to eat ramen noodles for a few days because you know it's part of your dream-making system. It's amazing how your perspective will change when you're working toward a specific goal.

Use this same process for all your goals. Let's say you want to buy a million-dollar house. The rule of thumb is that a home should cost no more than two and a half times your annual salary. Also, to avoid private mortgage insurance (and to increase your chances of winning a bid to buy the house), you want to put down 20 percent. Devise a system to save $200,000 and have a $400,000 annual income.

Dreaming about the house is the start. Creating a specific goal with a deadline is the next step. To make the dream a reality, you must put the systems in place and follow through.

DEVELOP SYSTEMS FOR EVERYTHING

Earlier, I mentioned Steve Jobs wearing his trademark black turtleneck, sneakers, and jeans. That was his *system* for getting dressed. It was automated to require the least amount of thought. You have a system for brushing your teeth, doing the dishes, and getting to sleep. These have all become automatic. I recently taught my oldest son the system for putting on cologne. Spray on left wrist, rub wrists together, then rub each wrist on one side of your neck. This will soon become automatic for him.

When I first started out in sales, I didn't have any systems. I didn't know how to prepare for the week, manage my time, or follow up with a prospect. I may have been at the office for twelve hours a day, but I only actually worked three or four. I was so disorganized that I spent half my day chasing my own tail.

Systems and technology go hand in hand. Even the calendar on your smartphone can be a huge asset. With any content management system (CMS), you can systemize your follow-up. A CMS like HubSpot or Mailchimp can easily automate specific emails to follow up with customers. And though fans of artificial intelligence will tell you otherwise, it doesn't mean that a CMS can *think* for you. You have to design the system to meet your needs.

Once you do that, you combine technology, delegating, and commitment to get things done. Maybe you have a system where, after every appointment, your assistant has a thank-you card on your desk with the address already filled in. You come back, and boom, without thinking, that card gets written.

As your team grows, you may need a new system. Some years, I have sent out more than thirty-five thousand cards. I couldn't handwrite all of them without my arm falling off. That's why I use a company called SendOutCards. I can say all I want about how much I care about making people feel special, but without the system I created using SendOutCards, I wouldn't have been able to deliver these special touches of gratitude and recognition.

I bet some of you have already identified systems as a weakness. It's common for visionaries and big-picture thinkers. It had been one of my weaknesses before I became a CEO, though I managed to work around it. Then, when I became a CEO, it didn't take long to see how it was a leak. If I had to start from scratch every time I gave a presentation, onboarded a new hire, ran a meeting, or delivered an annual review, I was going to be fighting uphill to accomplish dreams.

157

My dreams moved me. They got me out of bed ready to go to war every day. But without systems, I was an ineffective CEO. I simply couldn't outwork bad systems. As I mentioned earlier, I caught a break when the movie *Moneyball* came out in 2011. At that point, I was two years into running my company, and my lack of systems was becoming a liability. Because I had been so into baseball statistics as a kid, the movie finally gave me a new perspective.

Too many people make the mistake of thinking that most things depend on instincts and situational strategies. These types of people were depicted in *Moneyball* as the dinosaurs who fell behind in the race. The baseball scouts who failed to embrace analytics got replaced by those who relied on data (like Paul DePodesta, played by Jonah Hill). Instead of having the patience, humility, and long-term view to design systems and analyze data, the dinosaurs convinced themselves that there couldn't be a system to analyze players.

The equivalent in business are the people who don't think you can design systems for interviews, developing leaders, or making acquisitions. These are the same people who are saying AI isn't for them and that they'll leave it to the techies. They are in for a rude awakening. That's not to say that you never have to think or make adjustments, but that's the type of mentality that will kill your efficiency and prevent you from scaling.

USE SYSTEMS TO AUTOMATE BEHAVIOR

We have already discussed the importance of analyzing each quarter and updating your strategy. It's embedded into your business planning map.

Many things are in three-month cycles. Spring cleaning is great for both your personal and business life. As a reward for cleaning out your garage, treat yourself to a car detail. For your business, get the whole team involved, hire an artist, and after you clean and organize the office, have the artist paint a mural on one of your inside or outside walls.

Since we're talking about systems related to the calendar, one of the most brilliant innovative campaigns ever designed was by Jiffy Lube. As part of their marketing, they convinced people to change their oil every 3,000 miles. I was a Hummer mechanic in the army, and I can tell you that for most cars, you only need to change the oil every 7,500 to 10,000 miles. But what made Jiffy Lube's strategy so effective was that there was a system and a visual reminder. After every oil change, they put a sticker on your windshield with an odometer reading for your next oil change. You couldn't *not* see it. Imagine the systems it replaced: maintaining a database, direct mail or email, and couponing.

How can you create systems for yourself and for your customers? How can you get people to act automatically like Jiffy Lube did? How do you get yourself to take consistent action without having to think? What can you automate?

USE TRENDS AND ANALYTICS TO CREATE SYSTEMS

Peter Drucker, the author and founder of modern management, said, "If you can't measure it, you can't change it" and "What gets measured gets managed."

When you gather the data to track the viability of your systems, your systems get better. When your systems get better, achieving your dreams will become easier than ever.

You need data to answer the following questions: What trends did you notice? Were there spikes/dips in revenue/production? Once you've analyzed that data, how will you address these trends? You've done some of this work in chapter 2 when you looked at the previous year. The next step is to create systems to gather data, analyze it, and plan strategies based on what you've learned. The engineers and accountants love this section, and the visionaries are smart enough to see its importance. The audacious few understand that only with efficient systems can dreams be achieved.

Most businesses have some level of seasonality. That's why retailers have created events such as back-to-school sales and why online retailers created Cyber Monday. The problem is that this can create lazy thinking. Rather than create systems to address trends, too many people just accept that certain months are slow. Mondays and Tuesdays are your slowest nights at the restaurant. Do you just accept that? Maybe you close Monday to decrease labor costs and give your managers a break. Then you make Tuesday half-priced taco night. By the way, do you see how Taco Tuesday has become a systematic reminder for tacos? How can you create a systematic reminder that creates the type of consumer behavior that impacts your business?

Ski resorts in places like Colorado used to sell out in the winter and sit empty in the summer. I bet someone with a mission to create the best outdoor adventures had a dream to make active vacations fun. The next step was to have a goal of running a resort at 85 percent occupancy year-round. That's the big-picture framework. The next logical step was to analyze data. What months had the lowest occupancy? How were their competitors doing during those months? What other innovative campaigns had been used?

I know this is starting to sound like a marketing problem, but stay with me, and you'll see that we're talking about systems. The point is, you need a *system* to gather data, analyze it, and then build strategies. Too many people wait for problems to occur and then look for Band-Aid solutions. *The hotel has been nearly empty this week. Let's run some ads on Instagram and lower our prices on Expedia.* That's not a system; that's a shotgun reaction that occurs when you fail to plan.

If you're feeling some pain for not having good data, that's okay. It took me years of suffering without the right data to embrace systems. You simply can't write an effective plan without incorporating analytics.

Your first resolution as you start your new business plan has to be getting better at tracking data. If you're sitting here a year from now without a system to gather, analyze, and utilize data, you're leaving tons of money on the table.

Numbers to measure:

- Every month's record
- Every quarter's record
- Next year's goals
- Revenue/net profit
- New subscribers/customers

You need data to answer the following broad questions:

1. What will you measure? How will you measure?
2. What's your strategy for analytics next year?
3. What trends did you notice?
4. How do you create incentives to balance spikes/dips in revenue/ production?
5. Why will next year be different?

When I started gathering data at my insurance company, I changed the compensation plan and how we ran innovative campaigns. I invested millions of dollars in a proprietary software named Bamboo because of the edge it gave me. Data changed the way I managed, which changed our systems. As a result, we built a dream-making machine.

When you see a problem or an opportunity, I want you to shift your thinking from "We need a *solution* for that" to "We need a *system* for that." A solution is a onetime fix that requires you to keep reinventing the wheel and puts you in a reactionary place. A system is an ongoing activity that becomes duplicatable.

SYSTEMS TURN TIME INTO MONEY

A major part of systems is having the right people manage projects for me so I can be as efficient as possible. As a former mechanic in the army, I'm not afraid to get my hands dirty. In fact, I enjoy shining shoes and ironing clothes. It wasn't until I realized how valuable my time was that I had to stop doing these things myself. Then, gradually, I started asking, "What's the next thing I can have someone else do that I no longer need to do?"

The formula is the following: What do you know for a fact that your hour is worth? If next week you were able to find an additional ten hours, how much money could you make with that additional time?

If your value is $50 an hour, make a list of things that cost less than $50 an hour. If you can hire someone to shine shoes for ten bucks or dry-clean a week's worth of clothes for under thirty bucks, then find people to do that work. When I first started trying this, I wasn't fully sold on the concept that I could really replace those ten hours with what I was worth.

It takes a small leap of faith to start spending money on things you used to do yourself. It only took me four weeks to realize how valuable those hours were for me. As my hourly rate increased, so did the number of tasks I delegated. I went from one personal assistant to two. Now all I think about is how I can get my hours back to increase my efficiency. That's why I'm constantly in the process of finding strong project managers.

Project managers come in different shapes and forms. It's not just managing projects to develop a new technology, for example. It could be managing personal events. Birthday parties. Even health.

Doctor's appointments are a drain on productivity, especially when they are spaced out. That's why, for me and our C-suite, we do executive health testing. At places like the Mayo Clinic, UCLA Medical Center, or the Cleveland Clinic, you can see nine doctors in one day, from 6:00 a.m. to 5:00 p.m., instead of having to schedule nine different appointments over a span of six weeks and driving to nine different locations.

How many wasted hours have I saved by doing that? Counting driving time? Gas cost? Waiting nine different times for doctors who are not famous for being on time with their appointments? I would rather spend $3,000 to $5,000 to have it all done on the same day. I couldn't afford it when I first heard about this, but I was able to do it at UCLA when I was thirty years old. By then, my hourly value justified the expense, and I was blown away by the experience.

It all boils down to a very simple formula. Time is money. Systems save you time. Saved time makes you money. As part of your plan, keep finding systems that free up your time.

BECOME CHILDLIKE

I saved the most important question in this chapter for last: What makes you feel like a child again? What makes you feel like a kid on Christmas morning? How can you get to a place where you feel like that almost every day?

When I see a stale organization, a place where results have plateaued and people are going through the motions, I can instantly identify the culprit: the leaders have stopped dreaming. When that happens, everyone stops dreaming, and what stands in the place of an organization on a mission is a dull place where people dread coming to work every day.

For the greatest organizations in the world, the dream machine is always working. The leaders know how to move people. They constantly speak the dream language in a way that connects with people's emotions. Their imaginations run wild, and they become childlike. And, yes, there is a system to casting dreams. Decide on the rewards in advance. Make them specific and have a deadline. Find smart ways to measure them.

Dreams and systems, emotion and logic. Wash, rinse, repeat.

YOUR BLOCKS

DREAM

Action:

1. What dream gets you fired up? What specific words will you use to articulate this dream that force you to stretch, yet still allow the dream to feel attainable?

2. Declare your dream as a future truth and start to live in the present as if your future truth has already become a reality.

3. Convert dreams into goals by making them specific and measurable, with a deadline and a reward once you achieve.

4. Pay attention to your language. See if you are casting dreams at least 20 percent of the time when you are speaking to your team . . . and even speaking to yourself.

5. Make a list of five to seven statements beginning with "Imagine if one day . . ." and/or create a bucket list to drill down and find your true dreams.

SYSTEMS

Action:

1. Put systems in place for every quarter. Right now, go into your calendar and list two actions that will support your dreams in your personal life and two in your business for every change of season.

2. Put systems in place to gather, analyze, and implement data.

3. How can you automate your life and business? What systems will allow you to buy back time so you can be more efficient?

4. Find ways to buy back time. Figure out your hourly rate and delegate all activities that cost less than what you make.

CHAPTER 8

Culture and Team

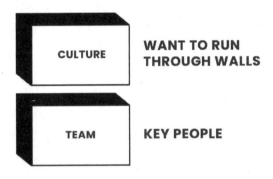

Culture eats strategy for breakfast.

Peter Drucker

I magine for a moment you're at a college football game in the United States that ends, in the final seconds, with a Hail Mary pass. The underdogs win. It's a huge upset. After the final whistle, fans storm the field in celebration and rip down the goalposts.

Why?

Because they've seen it happen dozens of times. That's just what people do to celebrate big after a game, which makes it a part of college football *culture*.

Though we tend to think of culture as an intangible, it's much more concrete than that. Culture, like religion, is rituals and traditions. It's the way we behave. If you run a business, you can't *say* you have a fun culture but have a bunch of uptight people quietly sitting at their desks in conservative suits. You can't *say* you have a culture of risk-taking but then fire or discipline someone who takes a risk. You can't *say* you believe in radical transparency, but then when employees offer constructive criticism, tell them their job is to be seen and not heard.

Culture is the sum of actions. At the 2022 World Cup in Qatar, when Japan defeated Germany, 2–1, it was considered a huge upset. A big part of Japanese culture is cleanliness. So what did the fans from Japan do after they defeated Germany in the World Cup? Instead of storming the field, like American college football fans might have, they grabbed trash bags and walked up and down the stairs cleaning up the stadium. The behavior was automatic because this ritual is ingrained in their culture, both as a country and as soccer fans.

Japanese defender Maya Yoshida said, "There is a saying in Japan that we must leave things cleaner than [they were] at the time we came to a place . . . That is one of the virtuous things fans are supposed to do. So that's what they did."

What happened next may have surprised some, but it made perfect sense to me. The fans from other countries started following Japan and cleaning up the stadium. After Japan's draw against Senegal, it was an incredible sight to see fans from both countries walking the stadium with trash bags. The reason it made sense to me is that **culture is contagious**. That comes from both consistency and recognition. When things get done over and over, they become the norm. And when people in an organization get credit for taking risks or even doing something fun like pulling pranks, others gain permission to do the same. Because the culture rewards those behaviors, they get reinforced.

By the same token, negativity and a bad culture are also contagious. Complainers love to recruit other complainers. That's why you have to keep a close eye on all the people in your organization. Ideally, you have mostly true believers who have bought into the positive culture you're trying to build and work to make it contagious.

WHAT YOU WILL LEARN IN THIS CHAPTER

As you plan your upcoming year, first think about the culture you want to create. That's a thought exercise, and it's worth gathering your leaders for a discussion. Then you want to *plan* the rituals and traditions that actually breed the culture that you say you want. There's a direct tie-in from your mission to your culture. Culture is your mission coming to life.

In this chapter, you'll learn exactly how to get people running through walls for you. You'll also learn how to choose your team: all the people you work with, from your inner circle to your C-suite to your employees to your vendors. Once you've built your team, I'll give you tips for choosing the people to run with, to let into your inner circle and help you accomplish your vision.

Choose a culture that suits your personality, and both your success and excitement will skyrocket in the coming year and decades to follow.

Culture Is What Defines You

Culture is having people wanting to run through walls for you and your organization. Culture is believing so much in a vision that people will do their best when no one is watching. It's also about *standing for something*. Let's play a game where we match an organization from the left column with a word from the right column. (Answers are below).*

Bridgewater Associates	Value
Zappos	Reliability
New York Yankees	Results
Armed services	Innovation
Costco	Radical transparency
Goldman Sachs	Honor
Lloyd's of London	Winning
Apple	Enjoyment

Now that you can see what it means to identify a culture, ask these questions to create your own:

- What defines your company culture?
- What are you actively doing to create it?
- How do you sell it to customers?
- How do you sell it to employees and partners?

---

* Answers: Bridgewater Associates = Radical transparency; Zappos = Enjoyment; New York Yankees = Winning; Armed services = Honor; Costco = Value; Goldman Sachs = Results; Lloyd's of London = Reliability; Apple = Innovation.

Skadden has twenty-one offices worldwide and is regarded as one of the top law firms in the world. Words to describe their culture are "relentless," "reliable," and "reputable." Their offices are decorated nicely, but not *too* nicely. They want their clients to feel trust and safety, but they don't want them thinking that *they* are the ones paying for the fancy art on the walls and over-the-top office decor. Sure, they'll take a client out to a nice restaurant, but they're not going to order thousand-dollar bottles of wine because, again, any smart client knows they are the ones ultimately paying for it. Plus, it suggests a culture of excess and waste—the very qualities that Skadden doesn't want associated with its brand.

Culture touches everything. How you decorate your office is a reflection of culture. At the former home office of my financial services firm, we rarely had clients there. A better way of saying that is that our clients were our team members. We had them in mind when we added a Ping-Pong table, a basketball hoop, and a state-of-the-art gym. That was all part of having an active culture. Just as I would often come in early for a workout, others would do the same. Many got into a routine of working out at 5:30 p.m., having dinner delivered to the office, and then working a couple more hours. Our culture supported this.

I love the question "Who do you want to be?" In order to identify and create your culture, you are answering that same question for your company. If you're a one-person business, who you want to be is all about you. It's the car you drive, the clothes you wear, the music you listen to, the books you read, your business card, your office, and where you entertain clients.

If you have a business, the question is "Who do you want your business to be?" In answering it, choices about your behavior—your traditions and rituals—will get answered.

MONKEY SEE, MONKEY DO

The win-win for this building block is that it's a lot of fun creating a unique culture. I enjoyed my office more when we installed a gym and added the basketball hoop. Just as I play music at events, I play it at the office. I'm also on both the giving and receiving end of a lot of pranks. And I can't tell you how many times I've dressed up to show how bought-in I am to a culture of having fun, being vulnerable, and embracing campaigns.

Culture is in the *doing*. It's the rituals and traditions that get repeated that create a culture. It really takes hold if the leaders and the CEO are leading the charge. If your culture values learning, bring in a speaker or workshop leader and provide a catered lunch. These "lunch and learns" build skills, morale, and teamwork. At a minimum, if learning is part of your culture, you must have a book of the month.

For a risk-taking culture, celebrate people for taking risks, even when that venture fails. Can you imagine standing up at a meeting and *praising* Debbie or David for losing the company half a million dollars? If you want a culture of risk-taking, you'd better feel comfortable doing that. You praise their vision, their process, and their courage for taking a risk. The fact that it didn't pan out is built into any risky venture. You explain that and encourage the rest of your team to follow their lead.

For a culture built on radical transparency, like the one I created for PHP (in part based on what I learned from Ray Dalio's Bridgewater Associates), you *thank* people when they offer feedback, even when it's critical. Then take it one step further and give them public praise for having the courage to notify a leader about their blind spot. In doing so, you let everyone in the organization know that the leader embraces criticism and uses feedback to get better. If people see that you and the other leaders in your organization can not only handle criticism but also *appreciate* it, then this behavior will be repeated and a culture of radical transparency spreads.

Your culture is going to be a reflection of you. I'm not a golfer or a drinker, so shop talk doesn't happen on the greens, and there isn't much drinking at events. No one has ever called me laid-back; I like being in the office early on Saturday mornings. Because I love what I do, I work insane hours. This also means that I'm available at all times to my inner circle, and most of the time to the rest of my team. It creates an element of safety and trust when people know they can reach you at any time. It also sets the bar for the company work ethic. People tend to copy behavior. They reason that if the CEO will take a call at ten o'clock on a Sunday night, they'd better be that committed as well. The flip side is that the companies I've started are also intense, competitive, and often lacking in work-life balance. It's by design that my companies are a mirror image of me.

Put this all together, and I create a culture that values safety, fun, playfulness, intensity, high standards, competition, and hard work. It's a reflection of me, for better or worse. Your company needs to be the same. If not, you're acting, and since **culture is ultimately what people do when no one is watching**, it has to be authentic.

ESPECIALLY WITH MINDSET, MORE IS CAUGHT THAN TAUGHT

Just as kids learn more from what their parents *do* than what they *say*, culture is the same way. **More is caught than taught.** Every action you take influences your culture.

Culture impacts mindset. It's one of the reasons I tip big. I'm demonstrating that I value hospitality, take care of people, and have an abundance mindset. Rodolfo Vargas, who I mentioned earlier, went from being flat broke working as a security guard at Sears to surpassing a seven-figure income in seven years and made it a point to tell me how much tipping influenced him. He said, "Watching you tip forty percent was an eye-opener. That's not part of my culture. Then I noticed how cheap I was with everything—not hiring assistants, not investing in my business, and buying cheap clothes. Even though I traveled a lot and lost a lot of time waiting in lines at airports, I wouldn't even pay a hundred bucks to get TSA PreCheck."

I knew Rodolfo had the talent and work ethic to be a star. I was in his ear all the time about his scarcity mindset, but words only have so much power. It took years of his experiencing our culture to change his mindset, which changed his approach.

Think about companies you've been a part of. Do you feel like they're being cheap with you? Do they cut corners? Do they send subtle and not-so-subtle messages about their culture? Drill down and get really specific about everything they do and how that culture impacts mindset. What time do events end? Is there a formal dinner or are people on their own? And where's everyone going *after* dinner—to the bar, the nightclub, or the gentlemen's club?

At a typical off-site event, we'll work until seven thirty, then have a phenomenal dinner from eight to ten, where the conversation really gets going. It's a given that I choose a high-end restaurant and pick up the check. That's a culture of taking care of people and rewarding them for hard work. At dinner, some people may order a glass of wine or have a drink or two, but since I'm not a big drinker, no one orders a bottle of wine or does shots.

After work or a work event, people will go to the *place to be*, which is where the key leaders are and where the real conversations take place. That place will vary depending on the culture that the leader has created. If, for example, you're a New York City firm in the finance or entertainment industry looking to recruit twenty-somethings who want to work hard and play hard (think *Wolf of Wall Street*), leading the charge to the club may be the perfect idea. There are plenty of people who look forward to company events as an outlet to drink their faces off. Unlike at Skadden, where ordering expensive bottles goes against their brand, for these companies, it may be a reflection of their culture. Sparing no expense and enjoying the finer things may be viewed as an alluring part of the culture for a hedge fund.

In my businesses, in which many of the leaders are couples, **people are looking for safety, career development, and relationship-building**. They joined the company to improve their lot in life and become the best version of themselves. To do so, they understand that they need to increase their knowledge and their network. After dinner, typically, we'll go back to my suite or the pool at the hotel or house we're renting and talk. Since the top leaders are there, no one wants to miss those conversations. There are no rules about what we discuss, and these are often the deepest discussions we have. Some people smoke cigars, but again, since I'm not drinking, no one else is either. We often go until three in the morning.

Imagine if you're the spouse of someone in the organization. Are you going to feel safe going to this type of event? How about when you can't make it, how will you feel about letting your spouse go? And how would you feel about recommending your sister's husband to work for this company? Then think about how you've felt in the past about other organizations, especially when they hold conventions in places like Las Vegas and New Orleans.

Be honest about your own identity and brand and how this impacts your culture. In doing so, you can be 100 percent authentic, have fun, and attract the right people.

BE THE THING THAT PEOPLE WANT TO BE A PART OF

People desperately want to believe in something. They also want to be part of something. Just as many people rely on their employer to provide health insurance, they look to their leader or their company to meet many of their emotional and psychological needs. At the top of that list are belonging, community, and esteem.

Talk to anyone who went to Harvard Business School, and they may share a dirty little secret. When they're somewhere and want to gain respect, they wait for the opportunity to drop what they call an "H-bomb." It's that moment in which they casually mention that they attended Harvard Business School. These are supposedly the best and brightest leaders in the world, and even they want something outside of themselves to provide validation. The very essence of name-dropping is to attach yourself to something of value to prove your worth. If you're an aspiring filmmaker not named Martin Scorsese, Christopher Nolan, or Quentin Tarantino, the next best thing is to say you work for them.

This explains why people are so loyal to their sports teams, and why in North America alone, the sports apparel market is expected to be $130 billion by 2025. Maybe you could never have played football for the Kansas City Chiefs or the Alabama Crimson Tide, but when you put on that jersey or paint your face with their colors, you're now associated with excellence. When you're on Wall Street and you tell people you work for Goldman Sachs or JPMorgan Chase, they will view you differently.

No matter how big a firm you are, you want to be more than **just** a business. **Just** is the word you don't want associated with your company. You want to build something that people want to be a part of. We hear the stories of companies like Apple and Google, but within your small world, you can gain that type of reputation. And in a world where talented people have choices, you'd better give them something to be a part of.

At Tesla and SpaceX, there's a culture of innovation. They're changing the world, helping the environment, and exploring new frontiers in space. There is also the halo effect of working for Elon Musk. When Musk took over Twitter in late 2022, he immediately tried to change the culture. He laid down the law, saying employees needed to be "hardcore" and "work long hours at high intensity." I have immense respect for Musk and figure this is likely to be move one in a series of at least fifteen moves to rebuild Twitter's culture.

Love him or hate him, Jack Dorsey did two things for Twitter. One, he made people feel like they were part of a movement. He said, "Twitter stands for freedom of expression. Twitter stands for speaking truth to power." Some of you may say that Dorsey didn't live up to this, but we can save that discussion for my podcast. Second, Dorsey believed in work-life balance and allowed much of the staff to work from home. This was impacted by COVID-19 and the turning of the CEO role over to Parag Agrawal, but still, it was the culture that Musk inherited.

Musk arrived, and if you believe everything you read in the mainstream press (which I don't), he dropped the hammer. Both Musk and the employees expressed how they felt about the culture. Employees showed it as twelve hundred resigned. Musk showed it by firing 50 percent of the workforce. When cultures don't match, there's going to be a lot of conflict.

When you're creating that kind of culture shock, not everyone is going to support your way of leading. You can either spend years to convert everyone or you can retain those who want to run with you and recruit new people who want to be a part of what you're building. For Musk, that means locking on to the people who get inspired by the idea of changing the world by protecting free speech and offering a virtual town square for debate and discussion.

There was an article on the *Forbes* website that painted a very biased view of the benefits of working from home. The article referenced Jack Dorsey's email to employees that they could work from home forever. While the mainstream media was pushing the benefits of working from home, business owners in the trenches, me included, understood the reality that you can't build a culture with remote workers. The press has tried to paint Musk as the villain in the narrative about requiring workers to return to the office, though most leaders I know agree with him. I'm not talking about solopreneurs and independent contractors like programmers who can work from home. I'm talking about building companies where talent feeds off one another and grows together.

No matter your industry or policy for remote work, you need to take care of people. I can say from experience that *especially* if you're going to drive people hard, they'd better feel five things:

1. They are part of something.
2. They are cared for and supported.
3. They are making a difference.
4. They are having fun and celebrating success.
5. They are being recognized for their contribution and feel needed.

As far as your plan goes, you can learn from some of the things I've done and study other companies. *Insider*'s list of the twenty-five large companies with the best cultures in 2020 had RingCentral, Zoom, HubSpot, Adobe, and Google at the top. Look at the five elements I listed above and make sure you are providing all five. If not, you're *just* another place people go to pick up a paycheck.

22 Ways to Build Culture

1. Encourage feedback so people are radically honest and transparent.
2. Make everything about how to make things better.
3. Pranks: they keep the environment fun and loose.
4. Have contests (at least monthly) to encourage competition.
5. Music: it energizes people and adds excitement.
6. Hire people who fit the culture. Don't force people who don't fit.
7. Add your personality and what makes you unique.
8. Create rituals and traditions.
9. Invest in personal and professional development.
10. Read together. Have a book-of-the-month club.
11. Celebrate birthdays and special occasions together.
12. Send personalized, handwritten cards for birthdays and important milestones.
13. Know people's dreams and create a merit-based system for them to realize them.
14. Get feedback from all sides of the company—genders, ages, experience, etc.
15. Surprise your team with spontaneous events.
16. Value leadership over titles. Titles matter, but examples of leadership matter more.
17. Recognize the right behaviors—give heroes the hero treatment for exceptional performance.
18. Allow for crazy things to happen—funny videos, etc.

19. Everyone has to be held accountable—and is subject to being called out.
20. Make high standards nonnegotiable.
21. Send meaningful gifts that show you know and care about the person.
22. Treat people so well that they don't want to leave.

THE MOST IMPORTANT VALUE IN YOUR TEAM

One of my most important values is learning new ideas and skills, so naturally, reading books and consuming content is important to me and the companies I lead.

I mentioned the trust versus performance video by Simon Sinek earlier, which reinforced my belief that people you can trust are more important than high performers who you can't. I wanted to turn the

RUNNING MATE SCORECARD

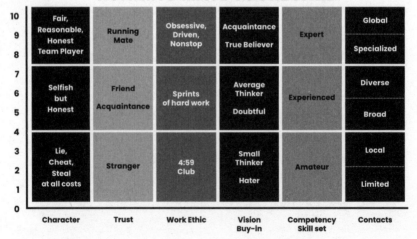

	Character	Trust	Work Ethic	Vision Buy-in	Competency Skill set	Contacts
10 / 9 / 8	Fair, Reasonable, Honest Team Player	Running Mate	Obsessive, Driven, Nonstop	Acquaintance / True Believer	Expert	Global / Specialized
7 / 6 / 5	Selfish but Honest	Friend / Acquaintance	Sprints of hard work	Average Thinker / Doubtful	Experienced	Diverse / Broad
3 / 2 / 1	Lie, Cheat, Steal at all costs	Stranger	4:59 Club	Small Thinker / Hater	Amateur	Local / Limited

trust/performance idea into something useful for my company and for anyone using this business plan. That's why I created a formal way to measure who you want to work with. There are six characteristics: Character, Trust, Work Ethic, Vision/Buy-in, Competency/Skill Set, and Contacts that you rank from one to ten. Then you total up the scores.

For your inner circle, people need to be high on trust. That's non-negotiable. Before I tell you more about other qualities you want from your team, let's talk specifically about your inner circle.

YOUR INNER CIRCLE IS THE BACKBONE OF YOUR TEAM AND CULTURE

You've heard that Jim Rohn quote a million times that "you are the average of the five people you spend the most time with." That's because both success and failure are most influenced by the company you keep. You naturally benchmark yourself against the people you're around the most. In addition, their activities, associates, and the books they read often become the same as yours when you share their circle.

Do you have an inner circle? If you don't have one, start thinking about who *you need to be* and who you want in this circle. You also want to make sure it's no more than five people.

There are two ways to develop an inner circle. The first way, if you're a student or just coming up in an organization, is to *find* the right inner circle. You have to identify the group of people you want to be a part of and offer value, so they want to include you. The second way is to create your own inner circle with high-caliber people. There are fourteen things to look for in an inner circle. You can also refer back to the Running Mate Scorecard and look for people with a score above fifty.

14 Things to Look for in an Inner Circle

1. Confidentiality: what's said stays in the inner circle.
2. Zero tolerance for games: manipulation leads to loss of trust, and trust is the foundation of the inner circle.
3. Accessible: easy to get a hold of.
4. Opportunity magnet: good attitude.
5. Lacks drama: doesn't see themselves as a victim.
6. Someone who gives insight (constantly teaches): shares insights on new books, interesting articles, and new ideas.
7. Pays attention to details: special touch and goes above and beyond.
8. Strong Rolodex and high credibility: they know people, and because of their credibility, these people take their calls and respond to their proposals.
9. Respect in their approach: the way feedback is given; the way they deal with others.
10. Defends you: tells you what's said about you behind your back; protective of the relationship and your credibility.
11. Dependability: you can bank on their word.
12. Exchange of value: not one-sided; picks up their share of the checks.
13. Fun and humble: zero tolerance for arrogance.
14. Presentable in appearance: never sloppy.

IT'S YOUR JOB TO PUT PEOPLE IN THE RIGHT POSITIONS

It may sound odd, but *there is a place for selfish people* in most organizations. That brings us to the two most common mistakes people make. The first is valuing competency over trust. These are people who create toxicity in the organization. It's hard to let them go when they bring in results, but if they kill your culture, you can't let them infect everyone else. These are the type of people that, once they're gone, you notice there was "addition by subtraction" because you can stop worrying about them poisoning the rest of the team.

The other mistake is thinking that every role requires the same traits. When you're building your team, you have to see people for who they are and then find their place within your organization. For example, I don't mind working with selfish people as long as they are honest. In fact, some of the best salespeople I know are selfish. All they care about is hitting their numbers. These people bring in a ton of revenue and are an important part of many organizations. I don't make the mistake of turning them into managers or leaders, and they're not part of my inner circle, but I can work with people like that. In fact, the more salespeople I have like this, the better it is for revenue growth.

Selfish versus selfless is such a delicate balance that I created a chart to better understand where I rank people. Reference it when you're building both your supporting cast and your inner circle.

I often talk about people who are in the 4:59 club. They can't wait to be out the door and won't give you an extra second when they're not on the clock. If you can trust them and they are competent, they're still valuable. If you let them be and accept that they do great work while they're on the job, there may still be a place for them in your company. Just don't try to turn them into leaders.

NET POSITIVE INDEX
"NPI" CHART

SELFLESS		SELFISH
0%	CRIMINAL/PSYCHOPATH/ DANGER TO SOCIETY	100%
10%	NARCISSIST (WORLD REVOLVES AROUND THEM)	90%
20%	SOLOPRENEUR/SETS AN EXAMPLE OF SUCCESS BUT BAD AT DUPLICATING	80%
30%	KINGMAKER/ DRIVER	70%
40%	SYNERGIST/ GREAT TEAMMATE	60%
50%	THINKER ADVISER	50%
60%	TEAM	40%
70%	PASSIVE/MEEK SUBMISSIVE/TAME	30%
80%	INDECISIVE/CONFORMING TO EVERYONE	20%
90%	WEAK-WILLED/ COWARDLY	10%
100%	MYTH/ NONEXISTENT	0%

Remember that this chart is a tool to *evaluate* people, not a way to *change* people.

The key to building your team is to accept people for who they are and put them in roles where they will thrive. If they're thriving, you're winning.

CULTURE IS PART OF YOUR "BENEFITS PACKAGE"

Unlike some of the other building blocks, you can't really separate culture from team. Though we label culture as emotional and team as logical, when people think about where they want to work, the lines between emotion and logic get blurred.

We tend to think of benefits as tangible things like health insurance and vacation days. As you plan to scale, I want you to expand the way you view your "benefits package." To me, it goes far beyond tangibles.

What are the benefits of working with you?

1. What benefits are you currently offering to others?
2. In what ways do people improve by associating with you?
3. How many lives have you changed positively in the past year?

Put even more simply, *do people around you win big?* If they do, build them up constantly and share their story of success with others. People will think you're a show-off if you're constantly bragging about yourself. But when you brag about the success of people who are associated with you, they will want to *join* your team. I can't talk enough about how Erika and Ricky Aguilar, who have no formal education and came from tough circumstances, became million-dollar earners before they turned thirty-three. I have dozens of stories like this, and I tell them all the time.

You need to answer the question: What benefits do you offer? By doing so, you will know how much value you are really bringing to people. If you don't like your answers, you're not going to attract people. If you're not attracting people, it's a sign you have more work to do to create success for others.

When I started my financial services firm in 2009, I offered no traditional benefits. Zero people would have followed me based on logic. Aside from a handful of support staff, every one of the sixty-six agents was a 1099 employee without any salary or traditional benefits like health insurance.

The sole list of benefits was associating with Patrick Bet-David. I look back at that now with so much humility. People had faith in my ability to create something from nothing and bought into my dream. They were buying me. They were buying a belief that aligning with me would improve their lives and change the fortunes of their family.

Does that sound logical to you?

Do you think I had a spreadsheet that analyzed revenue growth? We didn't have any revenue, and sure, I made projections about the future, but I didn't get into the nuts and bolts of the numbers.

You'll never be able to compete on logical benefits. Everyone can offer health insurance and free yoga classes on Wednesdays. Facebook was known for its over-the-top benefits, including free laundry, free food (with to-go containers), and free dinner if you stayed past six o'clock. Then, in March 2022, they eliminated the laundry benefit, took away the to-go containers, and moved free dinner to six thirty. At a time when people were losing faith in Zuckerberg's vision, instead of doubling down on culture and making the workplace a more exciting place, the company chose to cut benefits and reduce goodwill. Was this a case of putting short-term profitability over long-term value? Or was it a smart way to reduce expenses? Remember that we're playing the long game, and the impact of culture is felt over decades, not quarters.

Even the everyday things get taken for granted after a while. When you offer free laundry or free lunch every day, it doesn't add much to the culture, but it does add significantly to overhead. It's the surprise events and memorable activities that offer the highest return on investment. Make those events count and do them irregularly so they break up the routine and infuse your company with energy. You also want to have a good number of events that need to be earned. This keeps people excited and builds a culture in which success is based on merit.

Since learning and safety are such important elements of my culture, I plan events that build both camaraderie and skills. As I mentioned earlier, I spent $60,000 to put two of our teams through a two-day workshop on conflict resolution based on the book *Crucial Conversations*. People found their relationships improved not just at work but also at home. Because of that, the company got an immediate return on investment due to better communication. And people got an immediate return because they felt like they were part of a culture that supported both their business and personal well-being.

When I was looking to improve our team's culture in regard to accountability, excellence, and longevity, I thought about planning an off-site event to watch *Man in the Arena*, the ESPN documentary about Tom Brady. A company with an ordinary culture may have played it safe and aired an episode or two in the conference room. That's something that can be copied. I wanted to go big. I wanted people to talk about this for years to come. You can't put a price on this type of event, nor can you measure the impact in quarterly earnings. It's skill-building and team-building for sure, but it's also a recruiting tool, a retention tool, and a reward all wrapped in one. To make the biggest impact, I looked for the boldest venue.

How about Gillette Stadium in Foxborough, Massachusetts, where the Patriots play and the Super Bowl banners hang? Expensive? Sure. But not as expensive as offering free laundry every day. Once I planned the event, I created a contest, so people had to qualify. It meant more to people when they had to earn their way. Then I took it to another level by bringing in former Patriots players Matt Light and Rob Ninkovich for a Q&A as well as Ben Rawitz, one of Brady's closest advisers. People who don't even like football were riveted. It was a two-day case study in organization excellence. Because it was such a memorable experience, the impact on our culture is still being felt.

How will you plan to broaden your "benefits package" so that you don't have to compete on logical benefits that can easily be copied?

5 Reasons for Building a Great Culture

1. Excellence and high standards
2. Retention
3. Fun and excitement
4. Scalability and sustainability
5. Becomes bigger than you

REPUTATION IS THE KEY TO RETENTION

You need to make sure your talent wants to stick around. Retention is much more than a metric for HR. It's the way you build a company. If your team gets bored, uninspired, is doing the bare minimum, or lacks open communication, you will lose people.

It's expensive to recruit, hire, and train new people. It's also a drag on productivity because you're constantly having to repeat procedures. Worse, there's not enough time for rituals and traditions to take hold if your company is a revolving door.

Trillion-dollar companies like Alphabet, Apple, and Microsoft have all realized that a major part of their company's longevity has to do with how they make their people feel and the environment they create that their people look forward to on a daily basis. Before joining your company, people are going to do research. It doesn't take long for job seekers to go to Glassdoor or LinkedIn, or ask their network what they think of you and/or your company.

Questions People Ask When Deciding to Work with You

---

1. What makes your company distinct from your competition?
2. What separates your leadership from that of others?
3. Do you have a code of honor? Do you embody it?

How are people talking about you? What are you going to do this year, and every year, to both recruit and retain people? What rituals and traditions will you put in place?

BOLD MOVES BUILD LOYALTY

Many will advise you to play it safe but consider a different approach. Going against the crowd will make you stand out and draw the right people to you. If your values line up with the values of the people you lead, you won't have to worry about retention.

In April 2023, I watched the movie *Air* three times in one week—once with my kids, once with 55 employees of Valuetainment, and once with 120 sales leaders of PHP. There were multiple characters in that movie whom I related to. I loved Phil Knight's founder mentality, Sonny Vaccaro's audacity, and Michael Jordan's mother's unique negotiating style, which inspired a new way of compensating superstars.

One of my favorite scenes from the movie was when Sonny traveled across the country to Michael Jordan's parents' home in Wilmington, North Carolina, to speak directly with them about choosing Nike. He not only had to negotiate with Michael's mother but also had to convince Phil Knight to spend the entire marketing budget on one player instead of three. It was a huge risk, but it's part of the reason Nike became a company with a $170 billion valuation.

On April 22, 2023, the day after Tucker Carlson signed off on Fox News for the last time, I woke up at six a.m. with many thoughts running through my mind. Whether you love or hate Tucker, you can't deny the type of talent he is and the kind of loyal viewership he has. It's very rare that the number one superstar in any industry becomes a free agent. When that's the case, you have to capitalize and make a bold move.

Before the sun came up, I texted three leaders of our company—Mario, Tom, and Robert—and asked them to jump on an emergency call together. I told them, "I plan on making a five-year, hundred-million-dollar offer to Tucker Carlson. Let me sell it to you for ten minutes. Then I want you to tear it apart. Give me every reason not to do it."

After a half hour, we all agreed it was a good idea. Later that afternoon, I was scheduled to be on *The Megyn Kelly Show*. Since she and Tucker used to work together at Fox News, I thought it was the perfect opportunity to publicly announce the offer. Right after I made the announcement, I tweeted out the offer letter, which ended up going viral.

Dear Tucker,

I'll get right to the point.

We want you to partner with us in what we feel is a noble and necessary effort to define the future of media.

Here's our offer:

- $100M over 5 years.
- An equity stake with Valuetainment.

- President of Valuetainment and a board seat to project your strategic vision and voice.
- Your own podcast(s) and other daily/weekly shows.
- Documentaries and movies covering topics you care about.
- What else? We are all ears.

Our convictions about freedom, liberty, and truth run deep, and we believe we are the absolute right fit for you and America.

While we may not be the biggest media company, we are a new media leader driving into the future to make truth, fair debate, and commentary more accessible, consumable, and protected.

We are 100% serious about our offer.

Respectfully,

Patrick Bet-David

Needing to overpay people or offer best-in-class benefits is often a symptom of *not* having a strong culture, just like needing to have the lowest price is a symptom of not having anything unique about your product. You can pay people all the money in the world, and they still won't look forward to coming to work. A culture that fosters retention is when people say:

- I can't wait to be there.
- I'm making a difference and an impact.
- I'm having fun.
- The leaders are delivering on their culture's promise.

If you truly deliver on everything you say, you don't have to worry about losing people. The people who value your culture will find you. The ones who don't value it will filter themselves out. More importantly, you will retain the people you value and build longevity from a culture that continues to reinforce itself.

LOOK AT THE PREVIOUS YEAR TO IDENTIFY KEY HIRES

The next part of your planning process requires you to look back at your team from the previous year. Here are some questions to consider:

1. Who, in the previous year, proved they don't belong?
2. Who proved they can be trusted and should play a bigger role?
3. Who do I need to recruit?
4. Who (bookkeeper, personal assistant, etc.) allows me to buy back time?
5. Who (employees) allows me to grow?
6. Who do I need to collaborate with?
7. Who turns a weakness into a strength?

The first two questions won't require too much thought. The more important exercise is deciding what actions to take. It's not as easy as promoting or demoting people. There are more subtle ways of including them. A lot of it, for me, is about being included and receiving public praise. When I want someone to play a bigger role, they start getting invitations to my house and to exclusive events. I call out their accomplishments and allot time for them to speak at events.

What about the people who have violated trust or have taken a step back? First, I talk to them and see if they have learned from their mistakes and reformed their behavior. Then, until I see a change, I give them less attention and rarely edify them. When that happens, they either leave or up their game. Both are good outcomes if you want a culture that has high standards.

Your supporting cast should take stuff off your plate. They should help you double your time and never become a distraction or a burden. I can't believe how many people don't have personal assistants. Even if you can't afford someone full-time, you have to find ways to minimize administrative tasks or time-consuming ones that don't bring much value to the business. If you think a CEO's job includes going to the post office, and you think that means you're keeping it real, what you're really doing is keeping it inefficient.

In terms of recruiting, think of both offense and defense. Legal and compliance are examples of defense. Technology and analytics (data science) are both. Cybersecurity is defense. Better software that speeds up processes is offense. Analytics will help you see both leaks and opportunities. The minute you can afford to hire data scientists— or even if you're not sure you can—you need to hire these people. That could easily turn a weakness into a strength, just like hiring a great personal assistant will do for you if you're disorganized.

If your goal is to raise money, as mine was in 2017, you need to find the right investment bankers. But long before that, you need to recruit the right people for your team. I brought Tom Ellsworth into my inner circle because he had extensive experience in raising money. It allowed me to buy back time, turn a weakness into a strength, and determine which banks and investors to partner with. We ended up raising $10 million, which may have been less important than the partners we attracted and the value of their contacts and advice. This all happened because I made one key hire.

One key hire . . . Keep thinking about who can move the needle for you. In 2017, as growth was skyrocketing at my financial services firm, I knew that compliance was a potential threat for our organization. I identified Bob Kerzner as the key person who could turn a weakness into a strength. He was the CEO and chairman of LIMRA, the largest trade association supporting the insurance and related financial services industry, and had also been the executive vice president of Hartford Life. I invited him to join our board and asked him to audit our compliance. He came back with a forty-three-page report. Based on his findings, which revealed that we needed to play much better defense, I asked him to coach some members of our C-suite and to work with our carriers. It made our organization much better and reduced our risk significantly. All it took was awareness and humility to identify a key person who was strong where I was weak.

Contrast that type of humility with Sam Bankman-Fried, who has made the initials SBF synonymous with hubris and a lack of self-awareness. The headline on *Fortune*'s website on November 18, 2022, read "Investor Chamath Palihapitiya Once Advised Sam Bankman-Fried to Form a Board. FTX's Response? 'Go F—k Yourself.'" The subheading below it gave away the outcome: "The Crypto Exchange FTX, Once Valued at $26 Billion, Was Operating without a Real Board. Its Downfall Could Lead to Renewed Pressure for Private Companies to Have Independent Directors."

Your team is multidimensional. It's necessary for helping you address weaknesses or get ahead of potential liability. You'd better take responsibility for putting the best people around you. It's personal, business, legal, finance, family, and health. It's all of them combined.

ROCK-STAR PRINCIPLE

Since Netflix is such an excellent case study for culture, it's valuable to examine what they have done to build their team. Netflix cofounder and former CEO Reed Hastings follows the "rock-star principle": paying a significantly higher salary to hire one rock-star software engineer rather than hiring ten competent engineers. *No Rules Rules: Netflix and the Culture of Reinvention* by Reed Hastings and Erin Meyer is a must-read. It will change the way you think about who you hire and how you compensate them. Hastings writes:

> In the first few years of Netflix, we were growing fast and needed to hire more software engineers. With my new understanding that high talent density would be the engine of our success, we focused on finding the top performers in the market. With a fixed amount of money for salaries and a project I needed to complete, I had a choice: hire 10 to 25 average engineers, or hire one "rock-star" and pay significantly more than what I'd pay the others, if necessary.

Benefits of Hiring a Rock Star

1. Sets the tone
2. Raises the bar and brings out the best in others
3. Shows what's possible
4. Elevates performance
5. Expedites results

To hire rock stars, you must be a rock star: other rock stars want to join a team led by a rock star, especially one with the confidence to challenge them. This ties back to your "benefits package," and you'd better be able to answer these questions:

1. Have those around you made more money than they ever have?
2. How does your plan incorporate making others around you wealthy?

3. What do you want your top leaders/sales reps to make in the coming year? (Make a list for two to six of these top players.)

What benefits, both financial and nonfinancial, do others derive from being around your best self in the upcoming year and decades that follow?

FORMAL AND INFORMAL RITUALS CREATE CULTURE

Culture is about behavior. It's the rituals and traditions that turn into habits. I talked about how much I believe in learning and skill-building. Remember that it's not going to do any good to *say* you believe in education if you never pick up a book or don't spend money on training. That's like saying you believe in fitness while chugging a Slurpee and inhaling a jumbo bag of Flamin' Hot Cheetos.

Ray Dalio's views about radical transparency were a revelation to me, but I realized they might feel really confrontational to many people. In fact, when I later suggested making Dalio's book *Principles* our book of the month, several members of our executive team said we could not do that. I listened but felt strongly that this book not only had to be read, but also that its ideas needed to become part of our culture.

Those who brought well-thought-out ideas that challenged the book were heard. They added another perspective that brought fuel to the debate. Those who refused to read the book were let go. It wasn't personal. It was their way and our way of saying that we weren't a match.

Now, during the hiring process for every company I lead, we assign a book for each candidate. They are required to read it and come back with a one-page paper. It's a great filter for our culture. Better to know sooner rather than later if they are readers who are committed to learning. Based on that one assignment, we learn a lot about coachability and reliability.

Books are a formal part of our culture created by the leaders. It's also fun to watch informal rituals take hold. Some of these even become part of a firm's initiation process. Taking someone to lunch on their first day isn't memorable. That's why one of my favorite things to do with new hires when I lived in Los Angeles was climbing the Santa Monica Stairs.

After training, whoever was left at the office would gather to carpool to the Santa Monica Stairs. It was forty minutes from the office, and the car ride there turned into even more time for informal bonding. We learned what music people liked and got to see them in a relaxed environment. When we arrived, it was an intimidating sight to see the 170 steep steps that go up 110 feet.

The record number of round trips for the groups I took there was fifteen. A guy named Jason kept bragging that he would crush it. After his fourth one, he started throwing up. We had a big laugh, and that memory became a part of our culture.

Just like I'm a little weird, the companies that I lead take on that culture. We value fitness. We enjoy being together. The leaders don't think they're above the employees. By routinely going to the Santa Monica Stairs instead of going home or going to a bar, our culture got stronger.

I believe in high standards. No one ever won anything without high standards. That's why I call people out during Zoom meetings when I see them getting distracted. It's why I lock the doors at conferences and company meetings the second a scheduled break ends. I don't care if the people with low standards who can't be on time think I'm a hard-ass. I care that the people who are on time think that I set the bar high.

YOU CAN'T BE AUDACIOUS WITHOUT THE RIGHT PEOPLE

People want to go above and beyond because they know it will get recognized and rewarded. When I see people at the office who don't need to be at the office, I know it's working. People love being part of a team that cares about something and stands for something. Both the formal and informal rituals make a company unique and powerful. They also impact retention, which is a key driver of long-term value.

As for your team, think about who you want to hire to fit into this culture. Also, do everything you can to find high-trust people who allow you to buy back time.

YOUR BLOCKS

CULTURE

Action:

1. Choose the word or words that embody your culture.

2. Assign each new hire to read a book and write a one-page report so you can see how serious they are about working there.

3. Create an initiation ritual for new hires that embodies the culture, like a barbecue, hike, or sporting event.

4. Create rituals and traditions that align with your culture.

5. Build your reputation by being authentic so you retain the people who share your values.

6. Find people who believe in your culture. For example, it starts with you being the prophet evangelizing the concept of

reading books as a tradition in your company. Then you look for those you trust to promote this culture.

TEAM

Action:

1. Go back to your SWOT analysis and identify the key people you need to recruit to play better offense and defense.

2. Find rock stars who can elevate your company and happily pay them well above market rate.

3. Evaluate people hired on a scale from 0 to 60 using the Running Mate Scorecard.

4. Invest in developing the competencies of true believers lacking skills.

5. Hire people who allow you to buy back time.

CHAPTER 9

Vision and Capital

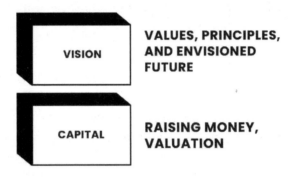

Good business leaders create a vision, articulate the vision, passionately own the vision, and relentlessly drive it to completion.

Jack Welch

A ship taught me a lot about vision. The Nimitz-class nuclear-powered supercarrier called the USS *John C. Stennis*, named after the U.S. senator from Mississippi, was built by Northrup Grumman for $4.5 billion in 1991. At 200 million pounds, it can house five thousand personnel. It is the size of three football fields.

None of those things make the ship all that special. But there is something that makes it so unique that I found a lesson about vision. For context, the average ship has to be refueled roughly every month. A special ship can last three months. How long do you think the *John C. Stennis* can last without refueling? Take a wild guess.

Twenty-six years!

What's the point? To me, the point is that if you have a strong vision, you don't need to be constantly motivated: you can go twenty-six years without needing to refuel. Just as the brilliance of the ship lies in its design, the brilliance of your career lies in your vision.

Imagine if you had a vision that fired you up without having to refuel for twenty-six years! It's no coincidence that we talked earlier about *The Toyota Way*; a typical Japanese business plan thinks about a business lasting for multiple generations. See how this is coming together?

There's a reason I saved vision for the last building block. Vision is what makes people never want to stop. You may see some similarities between dreams and vision. But the biggest difference is that dreams are more personal and have a timeline. You can fulfill a dream. A vision extends beyond you and your family. It's for the people you lead and the world at large, and it never stops. It's transcendent and will outlast even you.

For IKEA, the vision "to create a better everyday life for many people" provides fuel to never stop innovating. Amazon's is similar: "Our vision is to be earth's most customer centric company; to build a place where people can come to find and discover anything they might want to buy online." When Bezos stepped down as CEO, Amazon's vision lived on. There is no end date.

In fact, the only thing that can stop a vision is running out of money—aka capital. To get the money, you had better have a compelling vision and know how to articulate it to others. You also need to know your core beliefs and business principles. I'll share mine as a way to guide you to create your own.

WHAT YOU WILL LEARN IN THIS CHAPTER

In this chapter, we'll get into the nitty-gritty of how to raise money, and you'll see how vision and capital go hand in hand. We will get very specific about how to craft an elevator pitch, create a pitch deck, and present that deck to investors.

This chapter is going to be a little different than the previous ones. Because vision and capital both contain elements of emotion and logic, we're going to build the vision block in its entirety and then build the capital block in its entirety. Yes, vision is emotional, but it requires some very logical steps, which I will walk you through. And capital is really another form of sales. To move people so that they're willing to write you a check, join your company, or sign on as supplier, they need to be hooked emotionally and then taken through a logical plan. This is one logical building block that gets everyone excited! To make the vision a reality, you need money, and you need partners.

A STUBBORN AND SACRED VISION PRESERVES YOUR CORE BELIEFS

Authors, filmmakers, and content creators are looking for that holy grail in which their content is *evergreen*. More than twenty-seven years after they wrote the 1996 HBR article "Building Your Company's Vision," James C. Collins and Jerry I. Porras's explanation of why an organization needs a vision has held up:

> Truly great companies understand the difference between what should never change and what should be open for change, between

what is genuinely sacred and what is not. This rare ability to manage continuity and change—requiring a consciously practiced discipline—is closely linked to the ability to develop a vision. Vision provides guidance about what core to preserve and what future to stimulate progress toward.

Jeff Bezos put it more succinctly when he said, "Be stubborn on vision but flexible on details."

Did you get that? Do you know the core of your vision, and are you stubborn about it? Have you identified the nonnegotiables that apply to everything you do? If I get an opportunity that pays a ridiculous amount of money but isn't aligned with my vision, it's easy to say no.

The expression "When it absolutely, positively has to be there overnight" has become synonymous with FedEx. That vision guided everything. It created an obsession with logistics, technology, and systems. If it meant losing money for a few years or sacrificing the quality of the packaging, it didn't matter.

Speaking of delivery speed, in 1984, Domino's, led by then president Thomas S. Monaghan, created the thirty-minute guarantee for pizza delivery. They sacrificed quality and employee satisfaction. They also sacrificed driver safety. Everything they did, including how quickly they made the pizza, was designed to meet this vision. It proved to be successful in building market share. For that, I applaud Domino's. When you are laser-focused on one thing, your vision doesn't get watered down. In their case, the vision also became a liability because of lawsuits that came from drivers rushing to meet the deadline. When the guarantee had to be scrapped, the company was left scrambling to figure out its vision.

You could argue that Domino's lack of a *sustainable* vision opened the door for John Schnatter. I don't think it's a coincidence that 1984 was the year he founded Papa John's. From day one, Schnatter's vision was all about quality. He was so convinced by his own vision that he sold his 1971 Z28 Camaro to buy the equipment to make pizza out of a converted broom closet in the back of his dad's tavern. The next year, he opened his first store in Jeffersonville, Indiana.

Before I continue with this story, there's a good chance you've read about Schnatter in the media. I never shy away from tackling controversial topics or talking to controversial people. Because I had the chance to interview him on my podcast, I think there's real value in learning lessons from him about vision.

Earlier in the book, we talked about making your dreams visual for yourself. You do the same for your vision, except you expand the reach by constantly putting it in front of your employees, customers, and partners. For Schnatter, that meant using slogans internally like "Keep the Main Thing, the Main Thing," and "P.A.P.A." (People Are Priority Always). Of course, most of us have heard their ads, which repeat the vision over and over, "Better Ingredients, Better Pizza." It's no surprise that Papa John's was number one in customer satisfaction among all fast-food restaurants in the American Customer Satisfaction Index for sixteen out of eighteen years.

When I interviewed Schnatter in 2022, it was amazing to see how his vision was still seeped into his blood. He couldn't let go of his never-ending quest for quality pizza. As an experiment, we got pizza delivered from Jet's Pizza, Papa John's, and Pizza Hut.

Keep in mind that, at the time, the sixty-year-old Schnatter had a net worth of a billion dollars and had exited the business four years earlier. When the pizzas arrived, watching his intensity and attention to detail was incredible. He picked apart every last detail, from the placement of the pepperoni to the distance between the cheese and the edge of the crust. He explained what we could all see and taste— that Pizza Hut uses the cheapest cheese.

For Schnatter, "Better Ingredients, Better Pizza" was never just a goal or an ideal. It was a vision that transcended profitability and short-term goals. It was an obsession that drove every detail of the business.

Like Schnatter and many CEOs, Steve Jobs had to constantly choose between speed (or speed to market), cost, and quality. Sure, Jobs had to constantly make hard decisions and find difficult compromises, but the clarity of his vision of quality made those decisions easier. If a product launch had to be delayed or the price had to be increased, so be it. Quality, on the other hand, would never suffer.

What is sacred to you? What are your nonnegotiables? What vision can provide fuel for twenty-plus years?

ARTICULATING THE VISION

When I started my financial services business in 2009, I laid out a specific vision. I dressed like Doc (Christopher Lloyd's character) from the 1985 film *Back to the Future* to let everyone know that we were going to create our own future. When you're announcing a big vision, the setting helps. Where you speak and how you dress can amplify the effect.

Having a vision means answering these questions:

- How big are we going to be?
- What markets are we going after?
- What history will we create?
- Who is going to write about us and what will they say?
- How will the world look "one day" based on this vision?

When Steve Jobs was talking about the vision for Apple or Pixar, you'd better believe he wasn't saying, "We're going to have a local paper write about us one day." Now Apple is a case study at every university in the world, and one of the greatest writers in the world, Walter Isaacson, wrote a biography of Jobs. Steve Jobs didn't create Apple to get rich. The money was a given. But, without a vision, Jobs couldn't have created the foundation for a company that current CEO Tim Cook grew to a $3 trillion market cap.

Have you ever seen that video with Jack Ma when he created Alibaba in 1999? It's in Mandarin, but you don't need to speak a word of the language to *feel* his conviction. Thanks to the subtitles in the video, we know Ma said, "If we have that kind of eight-to-five spirit, then we should just go and do something else." And guess what he did to pour rocket fuel on his vision? I'll give you a hint. He chose his you-know-whats wisely!

To leverage the power of the enemy, Ma referenced Silicon Valley culture and then said, "This is the reason we dare to compete with the Americans. If we are a good team, and know what we want to do, one of us can defeat ten of them."

Articulating your vision attracts crazies, the type of crazies who will jump in front of a bus to see your vision through. These are people who want to be part of something bigger than themselves. They are simply waiting for a visionary to lead them there by painting a picture of the future.

A visionary is someone who can see things others can't. I had to see a world in which everyday people, regardless of their race, gender, or education, could be part of a culture that provided the skills, systems, and leadership to become prolific sales executives and entrepreneurs. I also knew that my vision had to be about more than producing millionaires. It had to have a cause behind it. I wanted to see the people I led become valuable citizens who helped advance the economy and improve communities. I had to see how success would become contagious and multiply. I had to see how the values and principles that

PATRICK BET-DAVID with GREG DINKIN

formed our culture would get so ingrained in people that they would lead someone from our ranks to become the president of the United States. (It has yet to happen, though my conviction that it will has only grown stronger.)

I saw all of it. No one else did . . . at least not at first. Most people don't see beyond their next meal, but man, do they love to jump on board when someone else can get them to see what doesn't yet exist. You have to have enough conviction and enough credibility to move people. A bit of theatrics helps to pull people out of their current state and cast a vision about the future.

Now that we've arrived at the final two building blocks, you're going to see some overlap with the previous blocks. Frankly, it's more important to build your plan than to make sure you put each idea in the right place. Like you do with dreams, when it comes to vision, you want to use the phrase "Imagine one day if . . ."

Imagine one day if:

- Entrepreneurship and financial literacy are part of grade-school curriculums.
- No one will have to use an insulin pump, and diabetes will be easy to manage.
- Seniors have peace of mind knowing their health care is taken care of.
- You can seamlessly connect to a world-class expert and be billed by the minute.

The first and the last vision statements are my own. I'll always be fighting for the first, and even if I can't change every school, by creating free videos, I'm constantly acting on that vision. The last one is for an app I created called Minnect. The key word is "seamlessly," because that definition will change as technology evolves. Even though we succeeded in realizing the "goal" of launching the app, the vision doesn't have an end date, which means we'll constantly be improving the user experience. My vision to give entrepreneurs every edge out there will never stop. I'll remain flexible on the products and delivery mechanisms, but stubborn on my vision.

DECLARE YOUR VISION AND WAIT DECADES TO MEASURE ITS SUCCESS

Having a vision is an essential part of your business plan. Your vision statement needs to check three boxes:

- Describes what you will create. It's the link between your imagination and the future reality where you change the status quo.
- Creates real impact on your customers and/or on the world.
- Clarifies priorities that ground all your choices and provide direction.

Once you have declared your vision, you only have to wait a couple of decades to find out if you realized it! Jeff Bezos had to deal with pressure from Wall Street when he was building Amazon. To his credit, he stayed committed to his vision and continued to invest in R&D at the expense of profitability. There were plenty of doubters at the time, and there were moments when Bezos looked foolishly stubborn. By staying committed to his nonnegotiables, he proved to be a visionary.

The jury is still out on all of us. You can't call yourself a visionary after a good quarter or a good year. Even a decade isn't enough. Leave it to Doyle Brunson, the poker legend who, up until his death in 2023 at age eighty-nine, competed at the toughest tables in Las Vegas, to offer some perspective. When Brunson was asked who the best younger poker players on the circuit are, he said, "Ask me in twenty years."

Success in business takes time. Anyone can go on a one-year run. Many people go on five-year runs. Only the audacious few go on runs for twenty years and beyond.

Being able to envision the future also means anticipating and mitigating regret. To be able to look back and feel fulfilled with your life twenty, thirty, or even fifty years from now, you had better have created a vision. I see value in getting a glimpse of what life will look like if you don't live up to your own vision.

See yourself, like Brunson, in your late eighties reflecting back on your life and career. Pick your favorite holiday when your family gathers. You're the grandparent or great-grandparent. If you had been on cruise control for most of your life, I guarantee you're going to feel bitter. You will be asking yourself, "Why the hell didn't I go all in? Why did I play small? Why didn't I take more risks?"

You're not going to share that story. You'll take it to your grave. And you are going to get more and more bitter as you age. The themes of your life will be wasted potential and regret. I think it's worth sitting with that feeling for a while. Taking the time to see yourself as a ninety-year-old will force you to see what your life will look like if you continue on your current course.

If you're more logical, or if you can't imagine yourself old and gray, another technique is to write your own obituary. That really will put your life in perspective.

Very few people can see beyond the present moment. An even smaller number can delay gratification in order to support their long-term vision. Then again, if you're reading this book, I doubt you consider yourself an ordinary person. You have a burning desire to be part of the audacious few. That's why I want to guide you to glimpsing future regret, as a way to get even clearer on your vision.

The moment you start fighting for something bigger than yourself—a true vision—you'll be introduced to a version of you that you've never seen before. No superpower matches this. None.

ARTICULATING YOUR VISION

Tim Ardam may be the most humble entrepreneur I know. His parents divorced when he was ten, and he joined the marines at seventeen. He was a truck driver and mechanic in the artillery. After his service, he worked odd jobs and then took a job with Power Plate in customer service and logistics. He started two businesses that failed and was in debt up to his eyeballs. Finally, he managed to start a company that worked and built it to more than $20 million a year in annual revenue, but he still felt that something was missing.

I asked him about his vision for the company, and he said, "When I started originally, I didn't have much of a plan. I just worked hard. In year twelve, I went to your workshop on business planning to plan out my 2022 and was expecting a very mechanical event, figuring you would walk us through the arithmetic for doing your numbers. I was blindsided, totally surprised by how emotional you got, and I realized that I had never had a vision."

As I said, Tim's business was doing more than $20 million a year in revenue, but he still said, "I struggled with vision. I was so used to putting every ounce of power to building. I'm definitely comfortable with who we want to be and where we want to go, but I had never really thought of the impact of vision on my company before."

Tim walked away from that workshop vowing to get clear on his vision. He told me after the event that he needed to create a vision board. But when he sat down to make it, nothing came to him. He struggled for months to clearly articulate his vision for the company or to define his most cherished values.

I'm telling you this story to show you that not all the building blocks get built overnight. Tim came back to the workshop a year later. Afterward, he called me and said,

At the end of 2022, I brought my wife to the Business Planning Workshop. I made all of my leaders watch the full-day workshop online. My wife cleared off a twenty-two-foot wall and made it a board to write on, and we wrote out our vision. I knew it was a hundred percent necessary to not just do a vision board, but also to get a hundred percent clear on our vision.

We needed to write down the justification for why we're all here. And it couldn't just be about the money. What is our dream? Why are we treating ourselves like the underdog? Why can't we see ourselves as killers who are just getting started? Let's do a highlight reel of the past fifteen years to remind ourselves how we got here.

We spent a full day working on it, and now we're closer with each other than ever because we share a common vision and know exactly what we value.

Since declaring his vision, Tim has seen a huge uptick in revenue. But, in the end, to know exactly how effective this exercise was, Tim—like all of us—will have to wait another twenty years.

CREATING THE VISION WITH YOUR TEAM

If you only write down your values and principles, you will get almost no value from them. If you print them and post them somewhere in your office, you'll still get little value from them. To create real impact, you must *ritualize* how they are created—only then will they start to inform your full vision.

My Business Principles

1. Never compromise our nonnegotiables.
2. Micromanage until there is trust.
3. What brought us here won't take us to the next level.
4. No one has 100 percent job security, including the founder or CEO.
5. Create positive peer pressure by challenging one another.
6. Beat your prior best.
7. Treat the company's money like it's your own.
8. Be radically open-minded but not easily persuaded.
9. Fight any temptation to lower expectations and standards.
10. Create an environment where our team is taken care of financially and professionally.

I repeat these values and principles so many times because I know they will eventually stick. A message heard once is not plenty. Repetition is how things get ingrained in people's minds. How many times do you think the slogan "Better Ingredients, Better Pizza" was repeated by Papa John's? Visuals help as well. In the foyer of my house, there is a massive painting with these words: Lead, Respect, Improve, Love.

Before I tell you what I did to create this list of principles and articulate the company's vision, understand that, for your own business, you can do amazing things on a small budget. Dressing up as Doc when I first started the business cost next to nothing, and it was still extremely powerful. In 2020, when my financial services company had a lot more resources, I decided to plow that money back into reinforcing our vision in an unforgettable way.

The entire event was a surprise. I told the team we had a meeting in Atlanta. From there, we boarded a private plane to Jekyll Island, a barrier island on the Georgia coast that was first discovered by Spanish explorers in 1510 and later governed by Juan Ponce de León. It's stunning. When you arrive, you can feel that it's dripping with history.

In 1904, the Jekyll Island Club was called "the richest, the most exclusive, the most inaccessible club in the world" by *Munsey's Magazine*. Members of the club included the biggest names in U.S. business: J. P. Morgan, Joseph Pulitzer, William K. Vanderbilt, Marshall Field, and William Rockefeller.

They decided to live (or vacation) in the same communities to raise children who became leaders. They created a place where other like-minded people could get away and mastermind together. We went to a historical room at the island's club resort and had a long discussion. Since it was a group of only twenty-eight, every voice was heard. They had all earned the right to be there.

Every detail matters at this kind of pivotal event. All of the men were dressed in navy suits with blue shirts and red ties, with matching handkerchiefs. The women were dressed in long, classic red dresses. We all made a declaration:

I. WE. NEVER.

I: Personal Responsibility

WE: Joint Responsibility

NEVER: Nonnegotiables

We wrote down our collective vision and our values and principles. We sent it to a professional editor. Again, every detail was covered. Once we had perfected every word, we wrote it out on a special
piece of parchment.

We recorded the ceremony and put up a private video for people
within the company to see. When we sent it out, the subject line of the
email read "Message from the Federal Reserve Room on Jekyll Island," and the video was titled "The Signers of PHP Agency." The
buzz and excitement around the video were overwhelming.

Now, fair warning, you can't invite everyone in your company to
this type of event. The people who don't contribute and don't have
credibility don't get a chance to participate. But for those who always
show up and are always all in, inviting them to define the company's
vision, values, and principles with you, their leader, will only deepen
loyalty and commitment.

Having a vision is infectious. It's felt by everyone around you. I
don't even want to tell you what this event cost me, but even before
I had to pay all the bills, I had already seen a huge return that went
beyond our income statement. It was an identity shifter.

There's another side to this. When you don't pay attention to principles and values, you will pay a price. According to the results of the
Net Positive Employee Barometer, which surveyed more than four
thousand workers across the U.S. and the U.K., the majority of employees aren't currently satisfied with corporate efforts to improve
societal well-being and the environment. **Almost half would consider
quitting if an employer's values don't align with their own,** and a third of
employees have already resigned for this reason, with these figures
even higher among Gen Z and millennial workers.

Former Unilever chief executive Paul Polman, who commissioned
the research, concluded, "An era of conscious quitting is on the way."

Do you think people are quitting because of too much money, growth, autonomy, teamwork, and fun? I doubt it. What they've really had enough of is a lousy culture, of feeling like a cog in the machine, and working for a manager who is going through the motions. Remember that **people don't quit jobs; they quit leaders.**

Many say we live in a time of transient workers who don't have any loyalty. That's a victim mentality. A winner's mentality is that because so few companies focus on values and principles, by actually creating a vision for employees to buy into, you can recruit and retain when you get it right. I encourage you to create a special event where you and your inner circle can define your vision and ensure its staying power. Here are seven guidelines to make your own:

How to Make Your Values and Principles Spread and Stick

1. Choose a meaningful place to create your values and principles.
2. Bring all the key stakeholders.
3. Allow everyone there to participate.
4. Narrow the list of values and principles to no more than twelve.
5. Make it your own with a preamble, or whatever works for your team's culture.
6. Create an impressive visual.
7. Put that visual in all appropriate places after the event.

HOW YOU PRESENT YOUR VISION MUST BE CONVINCING

Up until now, we've been talking about the inside world—you, your team, your family. Now we shift to the external. Yes, we're going to get into raising money, but we're going to start broader. What if you're trying to recruit? What if you're building a relationship with a supplier? If you're a homebuilder and you need a carpentry contractor, you're going to want better credit terms. You also want to be at the top of their list to get work done. To do so, you had better have a compelling vision and a plan that demonstrates your professionalism. The best-case scenario is people want to run with you. The worst-case scenario is that you instill enough confidence that people know they can trust you.

These days, it's not enough to be great at what you do. You need to be an expert at *presenting* what you do. Sure, James Cameron makes terrific films. But to get studios to invest hundreds of millions of dollars before he even starts a project, he has to present his vision for a film. If he doesn't nail the pitch, he'll never get up to bat.

Whether you're trying to raise seed capital on day one or you're trying to raise expansion capital in year ten, there's a right way to do it. It's the same process when it's time to:

* Recruit people
* Build early partnerships (suppliers, partners, etc.)
* Get a loan from a commercial bank
* Raise capital from investors

No matter who you are talking to, your vision must be convincing. Author Simon Sinek said, "People don't buy what you do. They buy *why* you do it." I want you to keep that in mind because even though much of this block is logical, it's the belief and emotion that spring from your vision that provide the fuel and win people over. You can have the greatest business plan in the world and the most detailed financial projections, but if people aren't excited, you'll lose their attention long before they see your plan.

DETERMINE YOUR "WHYS"

As Sinek points out, you need to understand and express the *why* behind your product or service. What you do and who you are is one thing. *Why* you are better is another.

Timing is everything. You'd better have answers for *why now* and be prepared to back that up with data. For example, you couldn't pitch Uber or Lyft until GPS and mobile technology had evolved to support the network. You also couldn't pitch an unbiased, down-the-middle news service until bias and polarity began to dominate the media. In fact, much of my vision for Valuetainment grew out of one-sided media that pushed an agenda and promoted outrage over objective debate.

Here are the "why" questions that you must answer before pitching your company.

Why Questions

1. Why is it different?
2. Why is it needed today?
3. Why hasn't it been invented yet?
4. Why is it hard to copy your idea?
5. Why are you the right person to build it?
6. Why is someone going to buy it?
7. Why will it hit revenue projections? (How big is the market? How many of those people are going to buy it?)

TO MAKE THEM "SEE," LESS IS MORE

Organize your thoughts and be concise. When raising capital, in some ways, a plan for investors is like a résumé. It has to be concise and fit on one page. It needs to use action verbs, highlight accomplishments, and be specific . . . without wasting any words.

It's amazing how people can be concise on a résumé and then become terribly long-winded when they're presenting their business plan. If they could, many entrepreneurs would jump at the chance to bring a portable whiteboard to a meeting! And, oh, how they love to wow people with acronyms and industry jargon. They think the goal is to sound smart when the real goal is to be *understood*.

You also want to use phrases like "Let me paint you a picture" and "Imagine one day if . . ." To cast a vision, you want to ignite people's senses, especially sight. You must make them *see* and *feel*.

The best way to do this is to rehearse answering key questions, using clear and concise language.

The reason we've been able to win is . . .

What customers love about us most is . . .

Our situation is unique because . . .

We're growing quickly because . . .

This is how I answered these questions when I started my financial services company.

The reason we've been able to win is . . .

Demographics and marketing have changed, and the industry has not. The average insurance agent is a fifty-seven-year-old white male who is uncomfortable with technology. Our average agent is a thirty-four-year-old Latina who grew up on social media.

What customers love about us most is . . .

They see themselves in us, and we relate to their needs. We re-fined our systems so there is less paperwork for the customer and the process is easy.

Our situation is unique because . . .

We limited our product to life insurance so we can recruit more efficiently and decrease the time and expense to become a moneymaker. Our customer acquisition costs are much lower because of how we leverage social media.

We're growing quickly because . . .

Our culture resonates with young, ambitious people, and we offer a path to financial freedom that's attainable and duplicatable.

Answer these questions and rehearse until they glide off the tip of your tongue. The faster and clearer you can express your vision, the more you will keep people's attention. And since I've prepared you for being concise, let's move on to the elevator pitch.

THE THREE ELEMENTS OF AN INVESTOR PITCH

The right story with the right examples gets people excited. There are three elements that you must nail.

1. Clear and Concise Verbal Elevator Pitch (THE HOOK that grabs their attention)

2. 15-Slide Deck (THE STORY presented with logic and visual clarity)
3. Compelling Verbal Narrative (THE EMOTION that sets your story apart)

YOUR ELEVATOR PITCH—THE HOOK

There's a great book on screenwriting by the late Blake Snyder called *Save the Cat*. His advice for a movie tagline is similar to that of your business pitch except it has to be even shorter. Imagine you're with your friends or spouse and are deciding what movie to watch. In less than seven seconds, the description should tell you what it's about and compel you to watch it. In fact, the biggest reason you won't buy a ticket is that you don't know what the movie is about. If the description uses words like "kinda," "sorta," or "resembles," it's already too ambiguous. *A legal thriller based on a John Grisham novel starring Shia LaBeouf and Emma Stone.* Say no more. Really, not another word.

Why, then, do you think people have twenty minutes, or even two minutes, to hear your business pitch? They don't, which is why you need to hook them quickly.

Why is a great elevator pitch important for any business to have?

- Forces you to focus
- Quickly tells the listener who you are at your core
- Calls for an answer

What is covered?

- The problem
- The solution

- The core differentiator
- Some statistics (numbers)

4 Rules for Elevator Pitches for Your Business

1. Understandable. Any investor, partner, or customer should be able to easily understand your pitch—no technobabble! Your listener shouldn't have to think too hard to understand it.
   - Somebody who is not in your industry should be able to follow the pitch. No buzzwords, acronyms, or industry jargon. Save those for internal meetings.
2. Quantified. Numbers win—size the market, state your sales, etc. Not just a concept. There are some proof points.
3. Succinct. The pitch needs to flow nicely in thirty seconds.
4. Compelling. The first three must state who you are, what you do, and why you win in a way that's:
   - EASY for the listener to grasp!
   - HARD for the listener to ignore!

Another thing Snyder recommends, which I echo, is to constantly test your pitch on people—those you know and those you don't know. Standing in line at Starbucks? Perfect! In between sets at the gym? Even better. Sweating in a long line waiting to go on a roller coaster? Make that time count!

When I tell people this, I get two objections. The first one is ridiculous, and the second one is rarely valid. The first is that the average person isn't smart enough to get their pitch. They are such geniuses that their pitch can only be understood by other brilliant minds who run venture capital and private equity firms. That's like James Cameron thinking every potential moviegoer needs a PhD in cinema to understand his movies. In fact, the opposite is true. As I said above, just about anybody should be able to understand your elevator pitch.

The second objection is that they don't want their idea to be stolen. This objection rarely holds up. Your *idea* is probably not revolutionary. Better ingredients to make better quality pizza is not the type of thing you need to copyright. It's the team and execution behind it that makes it bankable. When I hear people reluctant to share their pitch, the usual culprit is that they are hiding behind a fear of rejection. The bottom line is, if you're going to attract employees, partners, and investors, you must share your vision. If it's so easily copied, that may be telling you something.

To craft your elevator pitch, start by filling in the blanks:

My Elevator Pitch:

The problem: The problem we see/What's missing in the market/ What's frustrating people is:

The solution: Our company solves this problem by:

The core differentiator: What makes us unique and what allows us to win is:

Some statistics (numbers): We earn our revenue by:

A CASE STUDY: AIRBNB

Here's the story way back when Airbnb was a true start-up. (By the way, this is not a transcript. It was re-created by Tom Ellsworth, who helped me organize this content on raising capital and is still my go-to guy in this space.)

> Most tourists booking online care about price—and hotels are one of the highest costs when traveling. (The problem.) On the other hand, platforms like CouchSurfing have proven that over half a million people are willing to lend out their couches or spare bedrooms. (Some numbers to support market size.)
>
> We have created a platform that connects travelers with locals, letting them rent rooms or even entire places. Travelers save money, and locals can monetize their empty rooms. (Solution.) Unlike Craigslist, which is full of fraud, we provide the platform, insurance, and ease of booking. We then take a 10 percent commission. (Core differentiator.) With annual hotel room revenue at $122 billion in 2007, capturing only 5 percent of the market leads to $6.1 billion in annual revenue. (Numbers, revenue projections.)
>
> How does that sound?
>
> Would you be interested in hearing the full story? I can do it in less than a half hour at your office.

THE PITCH DECK—OVERVIEW

The next step is creating and sharing a concise presentation of fifteen slides with a compelling verbal narrative that's wrapped in contagious emotion. The pitch deck has three sections, all designed to follow the flow in a typical investor's mind:

Part 1: Problem, Solution, and Timing

- The problem:
  - What's the customer's pain point?
  - How do they work around or solve it now?
- Your solution (product/service and the magic that differentiates it):
  - How will you deliver value that fixes the problem or meets the need and makes the customer's life better?
  - What's the use case?
- Your business model:
  - How do you get paid?
- Why do this NOW?
  - What leads you to build it at this hour?
  - Are the customers ready?
  - What's the history that leads us to *this* being the right moment?

Part 2: Market, Competition, and Timeline

- The market you serve
- The competition: Who are they? Never say there's no competition. The consumer has had a work-around. Before Reddit, there was CompuServe and AOL chat rooms. Before that, there was the town square.
- The timeline: How long have you been doing this? What key milestones have you accomplished to date?

Part 3: Team, Financials, and the Ask

- Team: Where did you get the experience from? You'd better be able to explain your bio. You need to prove that you can execute.

- Finance: Results so far and the forward forecast. You need some results and a practical assessment.
- The ask! How much do you need? Equity, debt. How long will it last?

THE NARRATIVE DECK—THE EMOTION

One of the best things about the information and influencer economy is that there are so many experts offering advice. They tell you to follow their formula and may even give you a template to pitch your business (guilty as charged). The one thing I will not do, however, is tell you to do it the way I do it. Don't try to be like me, Steve Jobs, or Elizabeth Holmes. (Especially Elizabeth Holmes—unless you like the sound of prison.)

In fact, the number one rule for pitching is to *be yourself.* Stay within your personality. Authenticity wins. If you're a nerdy numbers person, talk about the numbers. If you're an engineer, get excited about the technology. If you're a football coach, bring a clipboard, give your best rah-rah pep talk, and slap them on the rear end a lot. Okay, maybe don't go *that* far.

Just be yourself. You want to strike that balance of being relaxed and confident while having a tone of urgency. Nothing should get you more excited than sharing your vision. If it doesn't excite you, it's not going to excite anyone else. Being excited does not mean being amped up with flailing arms and a booming voice. All you have to say is "I'm excited about this because . . ." and tell a genuine story that makes you excited. The audience will sense your sincerity.

Have a statement for each slide, like a verbal headline. Just like giving a keynote or a presentation, you never want to read your slides. Instead, make your words "color commentary" on the topic for each slide.

TEAM, FINANCIALS, AND THE ASK

What is my business worth and how do I come up with a valuation? That's the most common question people ask me. Look no further than the show *Shark Tank* to get those answers. The worth comes down to one thing, and it's not your numbers.

It comes down to getting others to believe in your vision. What are revenue projections? They are *guesses* about an uncertain future. How you tell your story will determine whether people buy into your guesses. (Estimates and projections are just fancy words for guesses.) Now does it make sense that visionaries are people who can get others to see a future that doesn't exist? The best visionaries can get others to write checks for hundreds of millions of dollars based on "imagine one day" scenarios.

I'm not going to get into the finer points of valuing your business here. As you plan for your year—and the next twenty years—you do need to figure out how much capital you need and how to get it. We talked about knowing your EBITDA, but especially for new businesses, there aren't earnings to speak of. Again, it comes back to selling your vision. Before you do make the ask, determine the following:

1. How much do you need?
2. What are you giving up, equity or debt?
3. How long will the money last?
4. What will it be used for?

If you tell investors that the money is for a fancy office before you have any customers, that probably won't fly. If you tell them it's to take a modest salary because you need to quit your job, selling that idea has everything to do with your presentation and what you've accomplished so far. The easiest sell is when you have existing orders and need capital to fulfill those orders.

In Alex Banks's Twitter post about storytelling tips that we looked at in chapter 4, he said, "Don't pitch to raise money. Pitch because you have never been more excited about what you could accomplish. Musk shows that Tesla can't do this alone. Receiving an investment comes as a byproduct of buying into your long-term vision."

Long before the ask, you need to sell your team and describe their track record of success in such a way that people will believe you can execute.

YOUR BLOCKS:

VISION

Actions:

1. Know the core of your vision and the nonnegotiables that will keep you stubborn.

2. Declare your vision and check all three boxes:
   a. Describes what you will create. It's the link between your imagination and the future reality where you change the status quo.
   b. Impact on your customers or on the world.
   c. Clarity of priorities that underpins all your choices and provides direction.

3. Imagine yourself as a ninety-year-old and, to help you see what you must avoid, envision what your life would look like with regret.

4. Organize a monumental event to create your company's vision, values, and principles.

CAPITAL

Actions:

1. Determine your differentiators: be able to explain all the "why" questions and what makes your differential advantage real.

2. Refined, concise elevator pitch: be ready to pitch at all times (like at the ER, in line at Starbucks, or waiting for the fire department!).

3. Crisp pitch deck: every slide (and every word) needs a clear purpose.

4. Compelling narrative: learn to create emotion by being yourself while presenting logically.

5. Respect the audience. Always, always, always walk in their shoes:
   a. Why should they be interested?
   b. Respect their time.
   c. Listen with your eyes and ears.

PART THREE

Bringing Your Plan to Life

CHAPTER 10

Assembling the Building Blocks to Make Your Own Plan

W e've been on a journey to find out how you become one of the audacious few. You've heard countless stories and examples. The goal was to get you thinking about your own plan. Hopefully, you've made some notes. If, however, you're one of those people who likes to take everything in before you start writing, you're still in good shape.

Now is the time to put everything together into one plan. Though I recommend that you write at least something in every block, it's more important that you make the business plan your own. Sometimes you need to learn the rules before you can break them. What will make your plan successful is that it feels like *you*.

The key word now is "distill." Less is more. Simplicity wins.

You want to break down your business plan into the smallest parts possible. Ideally, it will fit on three pages—a cover page and then all 12 Building Blocks on adjoining pages. That's about all your mind can take in. You may have some other items that will go along with the building blocks, like your calendar of events, in a separate place. I'm going to walk you through this process by first giving you the questions to ask. Then I'll show you an example. This will give you everything you need to fill in your own blocks.

QUESTIONS AND PROMPTS TO COMPLETE YOUR BUSINESS PLAN

The Year of _____ (Magic, Scaling, Growth, Clarity, Commitment—What's the One Word That Sums Up Your Year?)

This plan is for:

me

my team

investors

all of the above

This plan is for the _____ (calendar/fiscal) year and it builds the foundation for a __-year run.

Previous Year Review:

Biggest takeaways from the previous year are _____.

I allowed _____ to consume my mind. I will replace these thoughts with _____.

I will completely eliminate _____.

CHOOSE YOUR ENEMIES WISELY

I will not allow _____ to stop me.

This year will be different because _____.

Enemy	Competition
• The enemies that produce the most emotion are _____. • The specific enemy for this year for me is _____. • The specific enemy for this year for my business is _____. • When we crush this enemy, I am going to feel _____. • We will celebrate by _____.	• Key direct competitors are _____. • Key indirect competitors (alternative solutions) are _____. • I'm not going to underestimate _____ as they are a real threat. • I'm going to research my competition by finding a niche in _____ markets.

Will	Skill
• I will succeed because _____. • I must succeed because _____. • Tapping into my heart looks like _____. • I never want to hear _____ said about me. • I want my reputation to be synonymous with _____.	• My three areas of focus are _____. • I will read ___ books on these topics. • I will attend ___ conferences and workshops. • I will improve upon _____ (weaknesses) by _____. • I will make key hires in _____ (areas) to address weaknesses. • To hit next year's forecast, I need to add ___ skill sets. • I commit to personal and professional development in _____.

Mission	Plan
• The cause I am fighting for is ______. • The injustice I'm correcting is ______. • The crusade I'm leading is ______. • What bothers me is ______. • What I hate is ______. • What I love is ______. • If I won the lottery, I would commit my life to ______. • My mission is ______ *because* ______.	• I have completed a SWOT analysis. List one for each: Strength = ______. Weakness = ______. Opportunity = ______. Threat = ______. • The key people I'm watching are ______. • The key topics I'm watching are ______. • My crisis plan is complete. I'm prepared for worst-case scenarios and have anticipated crises such as ______. • My calendar for the year is complete, and I'm looking forward most to these three dates: ______.

Dreams	Systems
• The dreams that get me most fired up are ______. • My list of 5 to 7 "Imagine if one day ______" statements and/or bucket list items are ______. • Be specific and set deadlines and rewards for your dreams. • I have made my dreams visual by ______. • I declare my dream as a future truth and will live in the present as if it has already become a reality.	• I automate my life and business by ______, which allows me to buy back time and duplicate myself. • The 3 most important formulas in my business are ______. • My 3 specific strategies to drive consistent revenue this year are ______. • I have put systems in place to gather, analyze, and implement data. These are ______.

Culture	Team
• Our company culture is defined by _____ . • To actively create this culture, I _____ . • I sell it to customers, employees, and partners by _____ . • The rituals and traditions that align with our culture are _____ . • Our "benefits package" can best be described as _____ .	• I have evaluated key people on the team from 0 to 60 using the Running Mate Scorecard. My most trustworthy employees are _____ . • I keep people accountable by _____ . • I will find ___ rock stars for roles in _____ and happily pay them well above market rate.

Vision	Capital
• The impact I will make on my customers and/or on the world is _____ . • My key principles and values are _____ . • My nonnegotiables are _____ . • I will create a monumental event to create my company's vision, values, and principles on ___ (date) in ___ (location).	• My key personal differentiators are _____ . • My key business differentiators are _____ . • My elevator pitch is _____ . • I have a crisp pitch deck with a compelling narrative presentation. I use this when recruiting talent, building partnerships with suppliers and vendors, and raising money.

QUESTIONS AND PROMPTS TO COMPLETE YOUR BUSINESS PLAN

Solopreneur Example

This business plan is written by a solopreneur. Notice how this business plan incorporates both his personal and professional life; I encourage you to mix the two or to even make one just for your personal life, if that's what you need. Every business plan is going to be different. Again, the most important thing is to make it your own.

THE YEAR OF MAGIC

This plan is for:

Me

All the people I work with, my "team"

This plan is for 2024 and it builds the foundation for a ten-year run.

Previous Year Review:

Biggest takeaways from previous year: focus is key, discipline breeds freedom.

I allowed projects I wasn't passionate about to consume my mind. I will replace these thoughts with projects that light me up and make an impact on others.

I will not allow fear to stop me.

CHOOSE YOUR ENEMIES WISELY

This year will be different because I am committed. I know how terrible I'll feel if I don't keep my promises and how amazing my life will be if I do.

Enemy	Competition
• The enemies who produce the most emotion are the ones who are in the same field and beating me because they are working smarter than I am. • The specific enemy for this year is inconsistency. • The specific enemy for this year for my business is industry leaders who surpassed us in revenue last year. • When I crush this enemy, I am going to build a state-of-the-art home fitness center. I will prove them wrong by being my best self.	• Key competitors are other influencers targeting the same problems. • Indirect competitors are apps and DIY solutions. • I'm not going to underestimate the impact of AI and how it can commoditize information.

Will	Skill
• I will succeed because I'm talented, generous, and deliver value for people. • I must succeed because time is running out. I'm not getting any younger. • Tapping into my heart shows me that I want to make a big impact on the world. • I never want to hear "he has untapped potential" said about me. • I want my reputation to be synonymous with coaching, wisdom, and keeping promises.	• My three areas of focus are fulfillment, marketing, and relationships. • I will read 8 books on these topics. • I will attend 3 conferences and workshops. • I will improve upon acting small by being bold. • I will make a key hire, a marketing firm, to address my weakness in outreach. • To hit next year's forecast, I need to add AI, writing, and marketing skill sets. • I commit to personal and professional development in marketing, AI, and online training.

Mission	Plan
• The cause I am fighting for is living a fulfilled life (and showing others how to do the same). • The injustice I'm correcting is marketers succeeding at controlling people so that they make poor decisions. • The crusade I'm leading is being fulfilled. • What bothers me is seeing others unhappy. • What I hate is knowing what to do and not doing it. • What I love is seeing the light go on for people and watching their lives improve. • If I won the lottery, I would commit my life to guiding people to lead a fulfilled life. • My mission is to educate and empower because I care about people and have the experience and skill to make an impact.	• I have completed a SWOT analysis. Strength = Caring Weakness = Marketing Opportunity = New book Threat = Discipline • The key people I'm watching are James Clear, Andrew Huberman, and Joe Rogan. • The key topics I'm watching are influencer marketing and work-life balance trends. • My crisis plan is complete. I'm prepared for worst-case scenarios and have anticipated crises such as hyperinflation, supply-chain issues, and escalating marketing costs. • My calendar for the year is complete, and I'm looking forward most to these three dates: book publication, podcast launch, and a trip to Italy.

Dreams	Systems
• The dreams that get me most fired up are having an incredible partnership and impacting tens of millions of lives. • Imagine if one day: I have a home that feels like paradise and is also a retreat center; I host *Saturday Night Live*; I have a prime-time talk show. • I have made my dreams visual by creating a vision board. • I declare my dream as a future truth and will live in the present as if it has already become a reality.	• I automate my life and business by being hyper-organized, paying myself first with investments, and hiring a personal trainer, which will allow me to buy back time and duplicate myself. • The 3 most important formulas in my business are writing 1,000 words a day, posting 3 articles per week, and investing 3 hours per week in public service. • My 3 specific strategies to drive revenue this year are consistently writing a blog, building social media, and meeting all deadlines. • I have put systems in place to gather, analyze, and implement data. These are outsourced to a marketing firm.
Culture	**Team**
• My culture is defined by holistic health and the idea that everything matters. • To actively create this culture, I have a consistent routine and constantly seek out magic. • I sell it to customers, employees, and partners by embodying it. • The rituals and traditions that align with my culture are self-care, music, and bringing people together. • Our "benefits package" can best be described as: your life gets better because of my presence.	• I keep people accountable by speaking kindly, directly, and authentically. • I hold people to the goals and standards that we have mutually agreed upon. • I will find rock stars for roles in marketing and editing and happily pay them well above market rate.

Vision	Capital
• The impact I will make on my customers and/or on the world is guiding people to make decisions that create fulfillment. • My key principles and values are kindness, gratitude, love, and appreciation. • My nonnegotiables are violence, walking on eggshells, and being inauthentic. • I will create a monumental event to create my company's vision, values, and principles on July 10 in Sedona.	• My key personal differentiators are walking in other people's shoes and having unique experiences. • My key business differentiators are personal touches. • My elevator pitch is that I show people how to make better decisions to live a fulfilling life. • I have crisp descriptions of my website and marketing materials.

Now that you've seen an example, let's review strategies for how to best tackle your own plan.

Ways to Make a Business Plan Effective

1. Make time with your team and with your family to create the plan.
2. Know who you are writing it for (personal, your team, investors).
3. Make it emotional so it fires up you and your team.
4. Share it strategically—employ the right strategy to roll it out.
5. Build KPIs and incentives into your strategy and track religiously.
6. Make it simple enough for you to look at it weekly and not get bogged down.
7. Identify issues in advance and have built-in contingency plans and pivots.

8. Review it at the end of every quarter to study trends and recalibrate.

IT'S YOUR PLAN

The building blocks are there to provide guidance and structure. I'd rather see you write shorter, more impactful statements and plans than try to fill up space. We all have different goals and different agendas. Remember, there are no wrong answers. Keep it simple and find that balance of dreaming big while choosing goals that you can attain. Also remember that when you decide on the rewards in advance, you put yourself in the emotional state that will be required to overcome adversity.

CHAPTER 11

Rolling Out the Plan

The final test of a leader is that he leaves behind him in other men the conviction and the will to carry on.

**Walter Lippmann, American writer,
reporter, and political commentator**

You did it! Only the audacious few make it this far to assemble all 12 Building Blocks. You have a business plan. Because you've done what so few are willing to do, you are one step closer to building a multigenerational business.

Right now, you are probably excited. You are also probably alone. Writing a business plan, at least the first draft, is generally a solo endeavor. Running a business is not.

That's the good news. Even more good news is that I'm going to show you how to put all that hard work to its best use. You have the right blend of emotion and logic to make this your best year ever, as well as to make this the best year ever for those around you. Now you need a strategy to roll out the business plan to everyone who matters.

No matter where you are in your entrepreneurial or life journey, it's necessary and valuable to go through all the building blocks. The next steps will be different for everyone. Let's say you're a student who wants to drop out of school and start a business. The most important people to enroll are your parents, maybe for the simple fact that they're your best shot at free room and board. If you run a big business, you have to enroll everyone from investors to vendors to partners. If you're a sales leader, you have to enroll your team for sure, and you also need to enroll your boss—the one who allocates resources. Show him or her an incredible plan, and a big chunk of the marketing budget could find its way to you.

Your goal is to take everything you've written in the 12 Building Blocks and turn it into a presentation. You're not telling people about your plan. You are *enrolling* them in your plan. I chose that word intentionally. Enlist sounds too militant. Telling is too dull. Enroll means you are inviting them to buy in. When you have both emotion and logic covered, you don't have to sell. You simply have to share authentically to get people enrolled.

Steps Once Building Blocks Are Assembled

Here are your next nine moves:

1. Share it with one trusted person, ideally outside your organization, to get feedback.
2. Edit and polish the plan. Rehearse it out loud until you have it down cold.
3. Set up meetings with key stakeholders. Choose the locations wisely (outside the office is typically best, even better if it ties into your theme for the year).

4. Deliver a well-rehearsed presentation that balances logic and emotion. First tell them *why*. Then show them *how*.
5. Set key performance indicators and short- and long-term goals.
6. Agree on bonuses, prizes, and incentives for hitting goals.
7. Calendar out the entire year for everyone. Assign responsibilities.
8. Make the plan visual (laminate it, create signs and T-shirts, etc.).
9. Create regular intervals to gauge progress and course-correct.

Does that sound like a lot of work? Of course it does. Imagine spending days writing out the most detailed meal recipes for the week ahead. Would the work stop there? Or would it really *start* then? It's one thing to have the recipe. You still have to procure the ingredients, have the right equipment for your kitchen, and cook the food. And then you have to do it all over again the next week.

Or, for another metaphor, you've done the personal work to create this uncarved block of granite. Now you have to turn into a sculptor to refine it and bring it to life. You can't wing the rollout. You need time to let it sink in and make sure *you* are bought in before others will follow.

THE MORE THE MERRIER (AND MORE FULFILLED AND BOUGHT-IN)

Before we get into the details of the rollout, I want to tell a story that was relayed by a friend who went to Yale. In the first semester of his freshman year, he took a management course. As you would expect at an Ivy League university, the teacher spoke to the students as if they were going to become high-level managers. She asked what they, when they started in their careers, would value from their employer. At the top of the list were autonomy, upward mobility, and growth. Then she asked what regular employees valued. At the top of that list were pay, benefits, and perks like days off.

According to my friend, the Yale professor did a great job of getting the students to reflect. "Why do you think what *you* care about is different from others?" she asked. She shared statistics about how people at all levels of an organization value the same things. What she didn't say, but implied, is how these elitist eighteen-year-olds had so badly misjudged what *all* people care about. My friend may have walked into that room uninformed, but he walked out with the important lesson that people generally want the same things.

I bring this up because you may be wondering if everyone in your organization needs to create their own plan. The answer is that everyone should have the *opportunity* to do one. Don't you want to be part of a company, ideally leading it, in which every person takes the time to plan their success and gains clarity about what they want in life? I certainly do, and I can tell you that the more people who create a business plan, the better an organization becomes. The very reason I wrote this book is for everyone to have the formula to write a business plan.

Remember that most people don't have a vision and can't delay gratification. It's no accident that those things go hand in hand. Show people *how* to create a vision, and their discipline will improve. Is this effective for the custodian or receptionist? Ask it another way: Who wouldn't this be effective for?

Can you imagine asking your receptionist or intern, "Who do you want to be and what will your life look like in five years?"

There's a good chance that they'll tell you that no one has ever asked those questions before. Show that you care and guide them to answering those questions, and you may discover entirely different people. Their commitment to excellence will change, and not only will performance improve, but they may turn into true believers and flag carriers for your company. You can bet they'll tell their family and friends that you were the first person who took an interest in their future.

I asked one of our junior marketing people these questions. I had to probe a bit, and as you may have guessed, I asked him if he had any enemies or if there was anyone who doubted him. Then I asked, "Do you want to live a chill life, or do you want to make more money and advance in your career?" He said he just wanted to live a chill life.

The next day, he came to my office and said he'd barely slept. He couldn't stop thinking about my questions. He remembered how his uncle would always say he was never going to amount to anything, and though his parents didn't pile on, they didn't defend him either. When it occurred to him that the chill life would mean proving his uncle right, his perspective changed. That led us right into the building blocks, where we quickly identified the skills he needed to add to get to the next level. I asked, "What do you need to do to make that a reality? What hard skills do you need? What about human skills?"

All I did was ask the questions. His reflection and answers created the paradigm shift. Based on what I've seen over the past six months, I wouldn't be surprised if he's running the marketing department before he turns thirty.

If you think 12 Building Blocks are too much for some people, I've created a condensed version of the plan that may be more appropriate.

It's called the One-Page Business Plan, and you can find it in appendix B. You can also download a PDF and watch a video, "How to Write a One-Page Business Plan," by going to chooseyourenemieswisely.com. I'm only bringing it up now because I wanted to lead you, the audacious few, through all 12 Building Blocks. It may be handy for some of your employees, your interns, or even your kids. If, at any point, you sense someone is feeling overwhelmed, ask them to fill out the one-page business plan instead.

I can't say enough times that it's impossible to be a great leader without knowing someone's building blocks. I've been told by my peers that I'm great at pushing buttons. Well, how do you think I know *which* buttons to push? I ask people what their vision is, who their enemies are, and what people they are working for. I don't manage people to *my* dreams and goals, I manage people to *their* dreams and goals—the ones they have taken the time to write down in their business plan. Without gathering this data and taking inventory of a person's building blocks, you can't lead effectively.

SHOWING OTHERS HOW TO WRITE THEIR PLAN

As I said, the more people completing a business plan, the better it is for your organization. What you don't want is to assign a business plan without showing people how to do it. That will make everyone frustrated and it will feel like a waste of time.

It doesn't necessarily mean you are the person who has to lead the training. If, for example, you have a great HR director, he or she might be the person for the job. Since some people may be uncomfortable sharing with the CEO, it's best to have someone who people trust and will let down their guard with. You may have each department head lead it for their direct reports. If that's the case, you'll be leading it for your department heads.

The other key to this is to have examples, and not necessarily your own. People tend to struggle with blank building blocks. That doesn't mean make it multiple choice. What it does mean is that you want to give them prompts and examples, ideally from people they can relate to. When it comes to vision, if you say things like "take over the world" or "disrupt an industry," they're not going to know what to write in their own plan. Better to give examples like "I need to take a Udemy course on web design, learn conversational Italian, and save $15,000 as a down payment on a house."

I mentioned Bob Kerzner earlier. Not only was he the president of LIMRA and a member of my board, he was also the executive vice president for Hartford Life for thirty years. He taught me a lot about business plans. He understood how intimidating a blank page can be. That's why he created specific questions to guide people to their own answers when they were creating business plans. Kerzner said:

> Sales people are great at filling in numbers. I created a format that set them up for success. The numbers led them to their own conclusions on what activities they need to do. Ask the questions: "How much do you want to make next year? How much did you want to make last year? What do you have to do differently?"
>
> My format took them through what to do. By removing friction from the process, you get them to see for themselves what they *want* to do and what they *need* to do.

In a perfect world, you get as many people as you can to create a plan for the year. This includes your kids, your close family members, your personal assistant, and your vendors. In fact, supporting others in this process is a great way to make them feel better and gain goodwill as a relative, friend, and colleague.

TIMING AND SEQUENCING

One thing I obsess over is getting the sequencing of events in the right order. When you present your plan is critical. One route is to work with everyone to complete their own plan and then bring them together to share. In that meeting, you present your plan—the company's master plan—to everyone. Based on what you present, people on your team will likely be adding to their plan. If, for example, part of your vision is expanding to South America, someone on your team might take the lead on that, which will change their plan.

Assuming this is for the end of the year, the timing may look like this:

October 1: Announce location and date for business planning event in December. Announce date and time of business plan training in November. Make clear that completing the plan is a prerequisite for attendance.

November 15: Two-hour Zoom training on how to complete the plan.

November 22 and 29: Optional "office hours" to answer questions about the plan.

December 6: Zoom call from CEO about the importance of the plan. This is especially important if the CEO is not the person leading the training.

December 15 and 16: In-person workshop. One day is good. Two days are better. Off-site is good. Far away from the home office is better.

December 29: Deadline for visuals and to-dos from workshop.

The Following Year:

March 29 / June 29 / Sept. 29: Zoom for accountability calls and quarterly course-corrects.

Think about what type of business plans you've created and received in the past when you've gone through the motions or haven't provided directions on how to write the plan. Before I started teaching the 12 Building Blocks, most people showed up with a few bullet points on half a page. Now imagine putting that schedule together. No one would dare show up at your workshop without a detailed plan. First, they've been taught how to do it, and second, because of the "office hours," you've eliminated the number one excuse: I didn't know what to say. Plus, when your team sees how thorough you have been, they will follow your lead. Can you imagine following that schedule I just presented and not having the most killer plans that create the most killer year?

You have to make the timing your own. I'm providing this as an example of how precise and detailed it needs to be. If the most important part of your plan is raising money, the calendar is going to look a lot different. It might take months to make the key hire who will allow you to start working on a presentation and reaching out to investors.

The keys are:

1. Sequencing
2. Precision
3. Commitment
4. Leading from the front (i.e., you set the tone).

SELLING THE PLAN

Where you deliver the plan makes a big difference. What will create the most excitement? Sometimes you need to get away with your team. I've rented mansions in Palm Springs, California, and White Fish, Montana, a ski chalet in Aspen, Colorado, and the Oheka Castle on Long Island, New York.

When the meeting is finished, it's important to follow up on the items in a timely manner after rolling out the plan. Deliverables and next steps are crucial.

Why are all the details so important? People need to see that it matters to you. They will rise to your level of dedication and the importance you place on the plan.

Remember that you want to *enroll*, not enlist. You want to sound welcoming and inspiring. You want people to feel the energy pouring out of you. You need to sell the dream and explain the cause, all while keeping it simple.

Every salesperson knows that during a presentation, all the prospect wants to know is "What's in it for me?" The bad reps get bogged down in details or their own goals. The effective ones keep bringing it back to the prospect's needs and desires.

When you're selling your dream to your employees, you're selling what it looks like for *them*. You'll use those four magical words over and over: "Imagine if one day . . ."

What rewards will be theirs if you succeed? Show the impact on their money, career, history, legacy, and family. Describe what it will feel like when they meet a new, better version of themselves.

Keep that balance of emotion and logic. The building blocks were designed so this would flow naturally and all bases would be covered. You have to move people with emotion. At the same time, unless you provide logic, they are going to question *how* you will execute. Once momentum is created, you have a living business plan that will drive everyone around you.

DECIDE ON THE REWARDS TOGETHER

As a leader, there is always a delicate balance of gathering input and making your own decisions. For example, when it comes to creating a work-from-home policy, that has to come from you. Sure, you may solicit opinions independently and consult with people, but this is not the type of thing you want to bring to a vote.

One area where I like to gather input is rewards. When you set your BHAGs, ask your team what they would like when they hit them. For one thing, it creates the emotion of actually hitting the goal. You can imagine someone on your team (maybe your top sales rep) saying something like "When we crush our goal, we're all getting custom-made suits, Rolexes or Gucci purses, and flying to Jamaica together for a beach party with Ziggy Marley."

Then all you have to say is, "Is that all you need to crush that goal? I can't hear everybody."

You'll hear a big roar, and you know everyone has bought in. If you don't get that roar, you go back to the drawing board.

I find these are the best types of negotiations. You're pushing back some, but you're also smiling and challenging. As a leader, you may say something like "You really think you can do fifty-five million in revenue this year, John? And you really want that McLaren? How about sixty-five million and we'll do his and her McLarens for you and your better half?"

You're getting your people to dream. You're putting them in a place to visualize success. Of course you don't promise two McLarens if you can't afford them, but unless you're in a business where margins are razor thin, you'd love nothing better than to see a couple on your team do $65 million a year in revenue.

It's also a great place for challenges. When people declare their goals and others doubt them, it's the perfect time to tell them to put their money where their mouth is. They start making bets, and you get to play whatever role you want: "If Team A beats Team B, I'll buy three pairs of Louboutins or Ferragamos for everyone, and the losing team has to shine them."

In terms of the rollout, if your team is fired up, don't assume they are going to *stay* fired up and on task. Leadership and commitment to the plan has to be consistent.

A minimum of once a week, you need to be selling these building blocks, reminding your team that with the blocks, they can achieve the goals they've laid out and hit those rewards. You don't enroll people once and assume they're on board. It's constant. That's why you create visuals, laminate them, and make T-shirts with your word of the year. If your nature isn't to be a visionary, you won't wake up one day and think vision. That's why you put your vision in front of you and your team, and reward them as they strive toward it.

HOLDING PEOPLE ACCOUNTABLE

Language matters. Just as you speak the dream language and use phrases like "Imagine one day if . . . ," you also need a language of accountability. The right language gets the right results: "Where are you at? What's the status? Are you ahead of the deadline?" There's no magic in those particular phrases. It's the fact that you are asking the question.

Who holds you accountable? How? How often?

Who do you hold accountable? How? How often?

As part of your plan, you need to create accountability partners and checks and balances. Start by taking stock of how well you do this now. Are you good at holding people accountable? Why or why not? If you're not, the most common reasons are that you don't have the tools to manage conflict and/or you always want to be liked. In order to hold people accountable, you need to fix both of these leaks immediately, but both are necessary. You are welcome to copy a phrase that I use a lot, which is "You may hate me now, but you'll love me twenty years from now."

Rate how well you do the following (from 1 to 5):

____ Build relationships

____ Inspect what you expect

____ Give deadlines and hold people accountable

____ Develop mindsets

____ Lead from the front

____ Instill a competitive environment

IT STARTS AND ENDS WITH THE LEADER

Business plans and start-up businesses have much in common. People get caught up in the details, the presentation, and the technology, but what matters most is the people. Harvard Business School published a working paper called "How Do Venture Capitalists Make Decisions?" Here's a snippet from the abstract:

> We surveyed 885 institutional venture capitalists (VCs) at 681 firms.... In selecting investments, VCs see the management team

as more important than business-related characteristics such as product or technology. They also attribute more of the likelihood of ultimate investment success or failure to the team than to the business.

It's great that *Shark Tank* has brought entrepreneurship and valuation to the masses, though I think too many people make the mistake of believing that having a unique product or a patent is what matters most. It's not. What matters most is the leader. I don't invest in companies. I invest in leaders. I don't get excited about ideas. I get excited about entrepreneurs. I don't put my faith in technology. I put it in a CEO.

Just as a company will put a lot of effort into R&D to develop a product, for a business plan, we put a lot of effort into creating these building blocks. All twelve are important. But what matters most is you!

For your plan, you've figured out what makes you tick. You've learned how to buy back time and become more efficient. You've identified threats and leaks so that you can be your best. It's comprehensive because the only way for you to succeed is to be at your best—in terms of attitude, skills, organization, and energy.

How do you make this the plan that accelerates your business and takes you to an entirely new level? It's not one thing. It's twelve things. It's taking the time to look ahead in your life, to visualize both success and regret. You have to dream and tap into your imagination by constantly saying, "Imagine one day if . . . ," and then create the habits to make it a reality, all the while inspired by the visuals that are constantly in front of your eyes. Knowing whose ass you want to kick will keep the fire in your belly.

When you follow through on your own promises, you gain a new level of confidence. Others will see you differently because you carry yourself differently. It comes from an internal belief that you are living up to your own word.

A question I ask other leaders all the time is, "Can I cash your word?" If they don't get it, I'll ask the question another way. "When you say something, is it money in the bank, or will that check bounce?"

If people can cash your word, your credibility score goes through the roof. Your credibility score is like your credit score—it's a running record of every commitment you have made over the years. When that score goes up, you start believing in yourself. Confidence grows. Wins pile on top of wins.

And what happens to all those people who you stopped trying to change, who you stopped *telling* what to do?

Monkey see, monkey do.

By honoring your word to yourself and keeping your commitments, you *showed* them the formula. By delivering on the promises that you made to yourself and others, you demonstrated what it takes. That's leadership. That's what changes you and changes families.

———

Now that you know how prepared you are, I want you to shift your attention to getting the best out of others. For you to have your best year ever, a majority of those around you need to as well. The key to leading them is first to coach them on completing their business plan. Don't do it for them. Ask the questions and provide the guidance so they dig deep and do it themselves. It will make your job as a leader so much more effective.

It's impossible not to be reminded of what's important when you complete all the blocks. It also helps to have a leader to keep you accountable. When Jack Welch was working at General Electric as a junior chemical engineer, he wanted to quit. What stopped him from leaving was a mentor who talked him into staying. Twenty years later, Welch became the company's youngest chairman and CEO. Love him or hate him, during his reign as CEO the company ultimately increased its market value from $12 billion in 1981 to $410 billion when he retired in 2001.

What does Welch's story have in common with most? In just about every case, there was a *leader* in that person's life. Someone who believed in him or her. Maybe it was a coach, a manager, or a relative. Nothing lifts others up more than a leader who keeps his or her word. And that is why the leader is the number one indicator of business success.

As thorough as any plan is, no one can manage themselves (including you). People are human. They are going to have bad days. They're going to get off track. You have to be there to keep them focused. You must continually remind them of what's important to *them*. Depending on the person, you may remind them of their enemies or haters. Some people respond more to avoiding fear while others respond to achieving their goals. Knowing which is the sixth sense of any great leader.

Conclusion

Fu**in' bet against me. Bet against me. Tell me it's not going
to happen. Tell me it's going to fail. I love it. I love every minute of it.

Dana White, president of the UFC

O n March 18, 2012, on *60 Minutes*, Scott Pelley interviewed
Elon Musk about space exploration. Musk was forty-one at
the time and had a net worth of about $2 billion. There were
few believers in Tesla, which had a market cap of $3.6 billion, and
there were plenty of doubters about Musk himself. Many claimed he
got lucky when he made $180 million selling his share in PayPal to
eBay as part of a $1.5 billion acquisition.

During the interview, the energy was intense, as Pelley looked at
Musk and said, "You know there are American heroes who don't like
this idea. Neil Armstrong, Gene Cernan both testified against commercial space flight and the way that you're developing it. And I wonder
what you think of that."

Put most CEOs on *60 Minutes* and they look like robots. They
have been trained to be unemotional and keep an even keel. But with

Musk, you could immediately see the tears welling up. You could also see that he wasn't trying to hold them back. He responded, "I was very sad to see that, because those guys, yeah, those guys are heroes of mine, so it's really tough."

Pelley kept poking at this emotional wound. He asked, "They inspired you to do this, didn't they?"

"Yes."

"And to see them casting stones in your direction . . ."

"It's difficult."

At that point, Musk is really showing his disappointment.

"Did you expect them to cheer you on?"

"Certainly hoping they would."

"What are you trying to prove to them?"

"What I'm trying to do is make a significant difference in space flight and make space flight accessible to almost anyone."

I still get chills watching this interview. Now imagine if someone was interviewing you, asking you about your heroes, your heartbreaks, and your dreams. Would you get emotional? If so, what then would you *do* with that emotion? Even if you were moved emotionally, would you have a plan to channel that emotion?

In the decade following that interview, Tesla went from a $3.6 billion company to the second-fastest company to eclipse a $1 trillion valuation (it took them twelve years; Facebook took nine). Meanwhile, in 2018, SpaceX's Falcon Heavy carried a Tesla Roadster into orbit around the sun, as the first company to send a privately funded liquid-propellant rocket into orbit and land three boosters back on Earth. Then, in 2019, SpaceX became the first private company to autonomously dock in the International Space Station. Depending on what's happening in the stock market, Musk is often the richest person in the world.

We're talking about Musk because he realized his vision and his audacious goals. It would be wise to ask, what were the keys to his success?

Was it because he could identify his competition or because he had enemies (internal and external) that we didn't know about?

Was it because of his relentless pursuit of adding skills or his will to succeed?

Was it because he had a brilliant strategic plan or a compelling mission?

Was it because he created systems to scale companies or because his dreams were so captivating?

Was it because he assembled the right team or because he built the right culture?

Was it because he raised so much capital or because he knew how to get others to buy into his vision?

It's tempting to want to choose a side. It's natural to think in terms of either/or, emotion *or* logic. But we know better than to pick a side. Hopefully you spotted all twelve Building Blocks in the preceding questions and quickly understood that it took all twelve for Musk to succeed.

One question that's worth asking is: What came first for Musk? Did he have a logical plan to get to space and then use emotion to fuel him? Or did his desire start during childhood, when he was reading *A Hitchhiker's Guide to the Galaxy* while dealing with the emotional wounds of an abusive father?

When Musk received $180 million from the sale of PayPal, he had choices to make. Before he decided where to put his money, he had to know his vision and his plan. He could have chosen to kick back and celebrate his success, perhaps by sailing around the world or lounging on an island. Relaxing clearly wasn't going to satisfy his deepest why, which explains why he invested *all* of his money in three companies:

$100 million in SpaceX, $70 million in Tesla, and $10 million in Solar City. Did his heart follow his money or did his money follow his heart?

If I had to choose only one reason why Musk became so successful? He chose his enemies wisely ... and he keeps finding new enemies.

You build a great car: eight hundred horsepower, incredible chassis, zero to sixty in 2.8 seconds. But that alone won't get the car to move. You need something else to actually drive it.

You need gas. You need fuel.

Recruit your enemy and you'll find that fuel. Nothing else can produce that type of emotion. This is why you must choose your enemies wisely.

I've said over and over that a business plan first has to *move you*. Without being moved, without getting emotional, you won't follow through. The emotional current that lives inside you is a constant reminder of *why* you are working so hard. By knowing how to ask questions that tap into your deepest desires (just as Pelley did for Musk), your plan takes on an entirely new meaning.

I also believe that emotion alone isn't enough. Musk, like all of us, needed a logical plan that precisely detailed how to channel that emotion. Emotion is the *why*. Logic is the *how*. It leads you to specific actions that are required to start a business, scale a business, and put all the pieces together to design your dream life. If you take the time to write the plan and if you are committed to executing, you can change the course of your legacy.

By completing all 12 Building Blocks, you have passed the test. You are prepared to have your best year ever. Your best year brings you one step closer to your best life.

Entrepreneurship can be the answer for those seeking a better life. But it's hard. There are challenges at every turn, and none greater than at the beginning. Dreamers need guidance. Entrepreneurs need tools. Business leaders need a plan that is accessible and actionable.

When I went looking for the guidance and advice needed to write a business plan, it didn't exist. That's why you have this book in your hands. Once and for all, you have a complete guide to walk you through how to make your business plan succeed.

My why is impact.

My why is hope.

My why is using business to solve the world's biggest problems.

It all started for me twenty-one years ago when I chose the right enemy. If you're ready to build a multigenerational business, there's only one thing left to do: Choose your enemies wisely.

Acknowledgments

The bigger the vision and the bigger the challenge, the stronger the team you'll need. This book, right off the bat, was a challenge. Publishers said it would be tough to make a business planning book exciting. They also said that it would be nearly impossible to do exactly what I wanted, which was to write a book for people at all levels—founders, intrapreneurs, solopreneurs, sales leaders, and CEOs of Fortune 500 companies. I also wanted the book to be useful across industries—business, sports, military, sales, clergy, and politics. More than anything, I wanted to offer something that could change the game for the people I respect the most: entrepreneurs and anyone willing to get in the arena and compete.

What many saw as a problem, I viewed as an opportunity. If I were to ask you what the best book is on sales, you would think of a book right away. The same goes for leadership, management, and strategy. But if I asked you for a book on business planning, nothing would come to mind. That's because there's never been a go-to book about how to write a business plan. We decided as a team to take that as a challenge.

Writing this book required a special group of people. I was aware of Adrian Zackheim's reputation as the best publisher of business books. The first time I presented the idea to him, I could see that he was bought in. As excited as I was, he took the enthusiasm to another level and was already seeing ways to make the book better. This would not have happened without my agents, Jan and Austin Miller, who were with me every step of the way.

When I spoke to Adrian and his team, I was amazed by how meticulous they were with details. It took us six Zoom calls just to choose the right title. Niki Papadopoulos and Megan McCormack showed the same commitment to the manuscript.

One of the many reasons I value loyalty is that it allows me to buy back time. Since Greg Dinkin was the collaborator on *Your Next Five Moves* and Mario Aguilar and Kai Lode were valuable editors and contributors, they came onboard first. Three years after it debuted as a number one *Wall Street Journal* bestseller in August 2020, *Your Next Five Moves* is selling more copies now than after it was first published. Since I wanted to create another book that is evergreen, we assembled the same team.

On the personal side, the team was already in place. It all started with my parents, Gabreal Bet-David and Diana Boghosian. I wouldn't be who I am without them. Having my dad living with us has been an incredible blessing, and I'm thankful for every moment I get to spend with him. Our home has become a sanctuary. I'm so grateful to my wife, Jennifer, for supporting me since day one. She leans on Melva, who has been with us for fifteen years and is part of the family.

What makes it all worthwhile are my kids, who keep me energized. Patrick (eleven), Dylan (ten), Senna (seven), and Brooklyn (two) light up my life. It's also been great to have their cousins nearby. Grace (fifteen) and Sean (fourteen) are incredible role models, thanks to my sister, Polet, and her husband, Siamak Sabetimani.

Speaking of role models, there are only a select few who join my inner circle. Tom Ellsworth, the Biz Doc, and his wife, Kim, have become part of our family. When we were writing this book, my company was in the middle of an exit. Tom and I stayed up all night when we were in Monaco and had to make critical decisions with hundreds of millions of dollars on the line. When it mattered most, Tom delivered.

I can't say enough about Mario Aguilar, who has been by my side for eighteen years and is as loyal as they come. His wife, Barbie, has made Mario an even better man, and the birth of their son, Gabriel, has been a celebration for all of us.

I'm immensely grateful for the leadership team of PHP Agency, who bought into the vision I cast when the odds were against us. It starts with Maral Keshishian, the current president, and Tigran Bekian, a Swiss Army knife of utility who always has my back.

There's no way in the world we could have built an agency of more than forty-four thousand insurance agents without the heart, focus, and talent of our sales executives: Matt and Sheena Sapaula, Rodolfo and Cecilia Vargas, Jose and Marlene Gaytan, Jorge Pelayo, Jonathan Mason, Andrew and Jennifer Gaines, Ricky and Erika Aguilar, Chris and Vicena Hart, and Hector and Erika Del Toro.

I'm thankful for others in my inner circle, including Sam Carvajal, Leo and Clarissa Martinez, and Robert O'Rourke.

I wouldn't be writing this book or creating new content if it weren't for the millions of Valuetainers and entrepreneurs who follow us. I'm grateful to all of you. You energize me in ways that words can't describe. Special thanks to those who offered insight for this book, including Andy Beery, Tim Ardam, and Bob Kerzner.

I want to thank all my enemies. Those who have doubted me have a special place in my heart. I was tempted to list their names, since only some of them will recognize themselves in the book. Just know that I love you, and I'm extremely thankful for you. I chose you wisely, and now I'm off to new enemies.

Last, but definitely not least, I want to thank God. It's very easy to pray to God when things are not going your way. When things do start working out, it's easy to give yourself all the credit and forget about the endless nights you spent on your knees praying. I am forever indebted for the incredible blessings God has provided for me. The older I get, the more I understand why he wired me the way that he has. One thing is certain: I could never have built such an amazing life on my own.

GREG DINKIN

When people find out that I work with Pat, they always ask the same question: "What's he really like?"

I always give the same answer. "He's exactly who he says he is."

He never stops. He thinks bigger than anyone I've ever known. He sets incredibly high standards and elevates others to meet them. I've been lucky enough to shadow him for four and a half years, and the part I still find most fascinating is how he pushes buttons. For shorthand, I tell people that he's like Phil Jackson, the Zen Master. The trick is that he cares so deeply and listens so intently about people's hopes and fears that he knows which buttons to push. It looks like an art form to watch how he leads people to go beyond what even they think is possible.

I also want to thank Mario Aguilar and Kai Lode for being partners during every step of the process. They all laughed when I said, "I'm not a great writer, but I'm an outstanding listener and dogged rewriter." Because they offered detailed feedback, I was able to carry out Pat's vision and meet his high standards. The same goes for the team at Portfolio, especially Megan McCormack, who is as kind and patient as she is talented and insightful.

I want to thank our copy editor, Brian Kuhl, and our production editor, Randee Marullo, for her incredible attention to detail. I want to recognize the designers, Jen Heuer, Daniel Lagin, Brian Lemus, and Henry Nuhn. Thanks as well to an outstanding marketing and publicity department, specifically Heather Faulls, Esin Coskun, Mary Kate Rogers, Amanda Lang, and Kirstin Berndt.

I appreciate the support of my family and friends. Mom, Dad, Andy, Jayme, Drew, Logan, Thea, Levi, Phoebe, Michelle, Cully, Meul, Dreesch, Alec, Wilbert, Lucky, Cole, Wes, Hajjar, Nadia, Woody, Nicole, Rafe, Noelle, Rose, Monique, Jeremiah, Adam, Brooke, Andrew, Charlie, MK, Marc, Pastor Bob, Noah, Lori, Greg, and George all contributed in their own unique way.

Resources and Ways
to Stay Connected

For more information and helpful tools, visit:

chooseyourenemieswisely.com

MORE RESOURCES:

1. Since my Top 100 books evolve over time, you can always see what I'm reading: patrickbetdavid.com/top-100-books/

2. To learn more about consulting and live events, visit betdavidconsulting.com

3. Take a short quiz to learn what drives you: pbdquiz.com

4. For news, videos, and business lessons: valuetainment.com

5. To connect one-on-one with experts: minnect.com

Previous Year Review

- What took you away from your goals in the previous year?
- What could take you away from your goals in the upcoming year?
- What will you put in place to prevent (or at least mitigate) distractions and cut the fat?
- What important activities don't seem to get done? How will you fix this?
- What activities will you schedule?

1. Study trends
2. Good/bad/ugly
3. Month to month
4. Quarter to quarter
5. Missed opportunities
6. What you failed to anticipate (but should have seen coming)
7. Software failing
8. Hiring challenges
9. People quitting (Why didn't you see the signs?)
10. Supply chain issues
11. What you failed to anticipate (but could not have seen coming)
12. Black swan (unusual event)

What Events Have Consumed Your Mind over the Past Year?

- Relocating
- Company growth
- New office or return-to-office policy changing the ability to come into the office
- Getting healthy—low energy from poor habits
- Relationship—with current partner or looking for someone
- Kids
- High-maintenance employees
- Lawsuits
- Alcoholic brother who keeps asking to borrow money
- Fear about supply issues (without a plan to deal with it)

Cut the Fat

- What could weigh you down?
- What can you clear?
- How will you clear it?
- What actions will you take today?
  - Sign up for couples counseling TODAY.
  - Start looking for a personal assistant TODAY.
  - Hire a personal trainer TODAY.
  - Work on repairing your credit TODAY.
- What would your life look like if you got rid of distractions?
- If you want to do something big, you can't focus on the distractions:
  - One bad Yelp review
  - One former employee who wrote a bad review on Glassdoor
  - An event that should have taken three days to handle took three weeks

- Toxic relationships
- Unreliable vendors
- Make a list of the five to ten events that consumed your mind.

Rate Yourself on the Following (1 to 10):

____ Health/energy/stamina

____ Family relationships

____ Spouse/romantic relationships

____ Personal finances

____ Learning/personal growth

____ Spirituality/faith

Rate Yourself on the Following (1 to 10):

____ Hitting overall business goals

____ Developing leaders

____ Driving growth and revenue

____ Analytics and systems

____ Operations, tech, and logistics

____ Finance and managing cash flow

____ What did you do well?

____ What did you do poorly?

____ Why did you hit or miss your goals?

____ Did you overestimate? (wishful, delusional, lazy)

____ Did you underestimate? (playing it safe, not detailed enough to be accurate)

ONE PAGE BUSINESS PLAN

20___ THE YEAR OF_____

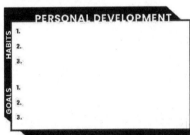

Notes

CHAPTER 1: THE 12 BUILDING BLOCKS

7 **There's also a belief:** Mike Puma, "There Is Crying in Football," ESPN, December 15, 2005, espn.com/espn/classic/bio/news/story?page=Vermeil_Dick.

9 **A big reason was:** Electronic Arts Inc., "EX-99.1 2 dex991.htm Press Release Issued Jointly by Electronic Arts Inc. and JAMDAT Mobile Inc.," U.S. Securities and Exchange Commission, December 8, 2005, sec.gov/Archives/edgar/data/712515/000119312505239198/dex991.htm#: ~:text=(NASDAQ%3AJMDT)%20today%20announced,total%20of%20approximately% 20%24680%20million.

CHAPTER 2: LOOK BACK TO CREATE DURATION, DEPTH, AND MAGIC

17 **I even made a video:** Valuetainment, "The 9 Love Languages of Entrepreneurs," YouTube video, June 21, 2016, youtube.com/watch?v=Vh-AN8m3LSs.

20 **According to Teschner:** Robert "Cujo" Teschner, *Debrief to Win: How America's Top Guns Practice Accountable Leadership . . . and How You Can, Too!* (Chesterfield, MO: RTI Press, 2018).

27 **According to the Centers:** Centers for Disease Control and Prevention, "Marriages and Divorces," National Center for Health Statistics, last updated January 26, 2023, cdc.gov/nchs/nvss /marriage-divorce.htm.

27 **Bureau of Labor Statistics:** U.S. Bureau of Labor Statistics, "Business Employment Dynamics," 2022, bls.gov/bdm.

30 **"Don't drink too much":** Joe Pinsker, "Japan's Oldest Businesses Have Survived for More Than 1,000 Years," *Atlantic*, February 12, 2015, theatlantic.com/business/archive/2015/02/japans -oldest-businesses-have-lasted-more-than-a-thousand-years/385396.

CHAPTER 3: THE PATH OF THE AUDACIOUS FEW

32 **"The generational curse":** Clarence L. Haynes Jr., "What Is a Generational Curse and Are They Real Today?" Bible Study Tools, March 13, 2023, biblestudytools.com/bible-study/topical -studies/what-is-a-generational-curse-and-are-they-real-today.html.

32 **"Sean just can't stop":** G. G. Allin, "Generational Curse," Urban Dictionary, June 11, 2021, urbandictionary.com/define.php?term=Generational%20Curse.

33 **According to *Forbes*:** Ashira Prossack, "This Year, Don't Set New Year's Resolutions," *Forbes*, December 31, 2018, forbes.com/sites/ashiraprossack1/2018/12/31/goals-not-resolutions/?sh =712d5a003879.

35 **Tom Brady said:** Jeff the Content Profit Coach, "21 Inspirational Tom Brady Quotes: Good Ones from the GOAT," *Medium*, February 1, 2002, medium.com/illumination/21-inspirational -tom-brady-quotes-a5db55cd9fd2.

35 **On episode 237:** *The Diary of a CEO*, "Chris Williamson: The Shocking New Research on Why Men and Women Are No Longer Compatible! | E237," YouTube video, April 10, 2023, youtube .com/watch?v=K2tGt2XWd9Q&t=1237s.

NOTES

35 **Students of Jungian psychology:** Louise Jackson, "Carl Jung and the Shadow: Everything You Need to Know," Hack Spirit, March 30, 2022, hackspirit.com/carl-jung-and-the-shadow.
39 **In 1984, Converse had:** Eli Glasner, "Ben Affleck's Air Ties a Bow on How Nike Cashed In on Michael Jordan," CBC, April 5, 2023, cbc.ca/news/entertainment/air-ben-affleck-michael -jordan-nike-1.6801736#:~:text=The%20year%20was%201984%2C%20and,market% 20share%2C%20followed%20by%20Adidas.
40 **When Nike signed Jordan:** Abigail Stevenson, "Nike Co-founder Phil Knight: Finding the Next Michael Jordan," CNBC, August 4, 2016, cnbc.com/2016/08/03/nike-co-founder-phil -knight-finding-the-next-michael-jordan.html.
42 **Nike defeat Goliath (Converse):** Trefis Team, "Was Nike's Acquisition of Converse a Bargain or a Disaster?" *Forbes*, November 15, 2019, forbes.com/sites/greatspeculations/2019/11/15 /was-nikes-acquisition-of-converse-a-bargain-or-a-disaster/?sh=24a60b8942f3.
42 **Nike became so dominant:** Gia Nguyen, "Most Popular Basketball Shoe Brands Worn by NBA Players in 2023," Basketball Insiders, April 17, 2023, basketballinsiders.com/news/most -popular-basketball-shoe-brands-worn-by-nba-players-in-2023/#:~:text=During%20the% 202023%20season%2C%20Nike%20was%20far%20and,covered%20nearly%2075%20percent %20of%20the%20NBA%20market.

CHAPTER 4: ENEMY AND COMPETITION

49 **ESPN's Max Kellerman:** G. Dunn, "Max Kellerman Says Tom Brady Is Done on First Take," YouTube video, August 8, 2016, youtube.com/watch?v=rcm1gnxpsMs.
50 **I loved seeing:** Sports Paradise, "Julian Edelman SCREAMS AT Tom Brady and Tells Him He's Too Old," YouTube video, February 8, 2021, youtube.com/watch?v=DLfP_kJ37E0&t=2s.
50 **During the 2023 NBA playoffs:** Taylor Wirth, "Fifth Steph Title Could Push LeBron Off Stephen A's Mt. Rushmore," NBC Sports, May 3, 2023, nbcsports.com/bayarea/warriors/steph -curry-could-replace-lebron-nba-mt-rushmore-stephen-smith-says.
50 **I'm not saying:** Valuetainment, "Stephen A. Smith Opens Up on Career Path to ESPN," You-Tube video, October 11, 2019, youtube.com/watch?v=p7hPgRT5vXE.
52 **His own coach:** Pete Blackburn, "Bill Belichick Has Reportedly Banned Brady's Trainer from the Patriots' Plane, Sideline," CBS Sports, December 19, 2017, cbssports.com/nfl/news/bill-belichick -has-reportedly-banned-bradys-trainer-from-the-patriots-plane-sideline.
54 **"10 simple storytelling tips":** Alex Banks (@thealexbanks), "Elon Musk is the master of pitching…" Twitter, March 11, 2023, twitter.com/thealexbanks/status/1634547220950429696.
59 **"ChatGPT May Be":** Aaron Mok and Jacob Zinkula, "ChatGPT May Be Coming for Our Jobs. Here Are the 10 Roles That AI Is Most Likely to Replace," *Insider*, April 9, 2023, businessinsider .com/chatgpt-jobs-at-risk-replacement-artificial-intelligence-ai-labor-trends-2023-02.
62 **"Let's say you pick":** Kings Inspired, "Become a Monster | Jordan Peterson—Joe Rogan— Jocko Willink," YouTube video, February 6, 2023, youtube.com/watch?v=ygEFX3ar2Qg.

CHAPTER 5: WILL AND SKILL

88 **Will is defined as:** *American Heritage Dictionary of the English Language*, 5th ed., s.v. "will," last modified 2016, thefreedictionary.com/will.
90 **"To get mathematical":** *PBD Podcast*, "Neil deGrasse Tyson | PBD Podcast | Ep. 223," YouTube video, January 9, 2023, youtube.com/watch?v=8hWbO9NdXbs.
96 **According to the *Harvard Business Review*:** "Reengineering the Recruitment Process," *Harvard Business Review*, March–April 2021, hbr.org/2021/03/reengineering-the-recruitment-process.
96 **"By the time I'm fifty":** Christian Zibreg, "Previously Unseen 1994 Video Has Steve Jobs Talking Legacy," *iDownloadBlog*, November 19, 2018, idownloadblog.com/2013/06/19/steve-jobs -1994-video-legacy.
96 **"There will be two kinds of":** Diamandis, Peter H. "Embrace AI or Face Extinction," Peter Diamandis blog, July 6, 2023, https://www.diamandis.com/blog/embrace-ai-face-extinction-exo.
96 **Ashton Kutcher launched:** Sam Silverman, "Ashton Kutcher Warns Companies to Embrace AI or 'You're Probably Going to Be Out of Business,'" *Entrepreneur*, May 4, 2023, entrepreneur .com/business-news/ashton-kutcher-embrace-ai-or-youll-be-out-of-business/451014.

NOTES

96 **These quotes don't sound:** "The Importance of Business Visibility and Online Reputation," Tomorrow City, March 29, 2021, tomorrow.city/a/the-importance-of-business-visibility-and -online-reputation.

103 **Study how Jeff Bezos:** Justin Bariso, "Jeff Bezos Knows How to Run a Meeting. Here's How He Does It," *Inc.*, April 30, 2018, inc.com/justin-bariso/jeff-bezos-knows-how-to-run-a-meeting -here-are-his-three-simple-rules.html.

107 **"It's not that":** brainyquote.com/quotes/albert_einstein_10619.

109 **Navy SEALs and how they value:** Gabe Villamizer, "Simon Sinek—Trust vs. Performance (Must Watch!)," YouTube video, November 17, 2022, youtube.com/watch?v=PTo9e3ILmms.

111 **Henry Ford said:** Noah Marks, "Two Undeniable Truths in Quotes," LinkedIn, May 14, 2020, linkedin.com/pulse/two-undeniable-truths-quotes-noah-marks

111 **Richard Branson said:** Richard Branson (@RichardBranson), "Train people well enough so they can leave, treat them well enough so they don't want to," Twitter, March 27, 2014, twitter .com/richardbranson/status/449220072176107520?lang=en.

CHAPTER 6: MISSION AND PLAN

115 **"A small body of determined":** "Mahatma Gandhi Quotes," Allauthor.com, retrieved June 22, 2023, allauthor.com/quote/40507/.

120 **According to *Inc.*:** Dan Whateley, "People Laughed When She Wanted to Take On a Common (but Totally Embarrassing) Problem. Now She Has a $400 Million Business," *Inc.*, June 20, 2019, inc.com/dan-whateley/poo-pourri-suzy-batiz-bathroom-odor-oversharing.html.

122 **"perhaps the most powerful":** Wikipedia, s.v. "George Will," last modified May 23, 2023, en.wikipedia.org/wiki/George_Will.

127 **Ellen Langer, a Harvard psychologist:** Susan Weinschenk, "The Power of the Word 'Because' to Get People to Do Stuff," *Psychology Today*, October 15, 2013, psychologytoday .com/us/blog/brain-wise/201310/the-power-of-the-word-because-to-get-people-to-do -stuff.

135 **When I interviewed him:** Valuetainment, "Kobe Bryant's Last Great Interview," YouTube video, August 23, 2019, youtube.com/watch?v=T9GvDekiJ9c&t=1s.

136 **Seth Godin, author of numerous:** Seth Godin, "Project Management," *Seth's Blog*, June 21, 2023, https://seths.blog/.

136 **Dwight D. Eisenhower said:** Richard Nixon, "Khrushchev," *Six Crises* (New York: Simon & Schuster, 1962).

136 **Ike wasn't quite:** Greg Young, "Proper Planning and Preparation Prevent Piss Poor Performance (the 7Ps)," LinkedIn, April 8, 2020, linkedin.com/pulse/proper-planning-preparation -prevent-piss-poor-7ps-greg-young.

CHAPTER 7: DREAMS AND SYSTEMS

158 **The baseball scouts:** Colin McCormick and Gabriel Ponniah, "Moneyball: What Happened to Paul DePodesta (The Real Peter Brand)," May 24, 2023, screenrant.com/moneyball-peter-brand -paul-depodesta-what-happened.

CHAPTER 8: CULTURE AND TEAM

176 **This explains why people:** P. Smith, "Value of the Sportswear Market in the United States from 2019 to 2025," Statista, April 27, 2022, statista.com/statistics/1087137/value-of-the-sports -apparel-market-by-product-category-us.

177 **He said, "Twitter stands for":** Matt Weinberger, "Jack Dorsey: 'Twitter Stands for Freedom of Expression,'" Yahoo, October 21, 2015, yahoo.com/lifestyle/s/jack-dorsey-twitter-stands -freedom-175932575.html.

178 **There was an article:** Jack Kelly, "Twitter CEO Jack Dorsey Tells Employees They Can Work from Home 'Forever'—Before You Celebrate, There's a Catch," *Forbes*, May 13, 2020, forbes.com/sites/jackkelly/2020/05/13/twitter-ceo-jack-dorsey-tells-employees-they-can -work-from-home-forever-before-you-celebrate-theres-a-catch/?sh=28eca17f2e91.

178 ***Insider's* list of the twenty-five:** Madison Hoff, "The 25 Large Companies with the Best

NOTES

Culture in 2020," *Insider*, December 14, 2020, businessinsider.com/large-companies-best-culture-comparably-2020-12.

186 **Then, in March 2022:** Nathan Solis, "Facebook Company Ends Its Free Laundry Perk, and at Least One Worker Is Steamed," *Los Angeles Times*, March 16, 2022, latimes.com/california/story/2022-03-16/facebook-company-meta-ends-its-free-laundry-perk#:~:text=Facebook%20company%20ends%20its%20free,%2C%20Calif.%2C%20last%20year.

194 **The headline on *Fortune*'s website:** Lila Maclellan, "Investor Chamath Palihapitiya Once Advised Sam Bankman-Fried to Form a Board. FTX's Response? 'Go F—k Yourself,'" *Fortune*, November 18, 2022, fortune.com/2022/11/18/ftx-board-investor-chamath-palihapitiya-sam-bankman-fried-board-directors-crypto.

195 **"In the first few years":** Reeds Hastings, "Netflix CEO on Paying Sky-High Salaries: 'The Best are Easily 10 Times Better Than Average,'" CNBC, September 8, 2020, cnbc.com/2020/09/08/netflix-ceo-reed-hastings-on-high-salaries-the-best-are-easily-10x-better-than-average.html.

CHAPTER 9: VISION AND CAPITAL

202 **For IKEA, the vision:** Daniel Pereira, "IKEA Mission and Vision Statement," The Business Model Analyst, April 24, 2023, businessmodelanalyst.com/ikea-mission-and-vision-statement/.

202 **Amazon's is similar:** Patrick Hull, "Be Visionary. Think Big," *Forbes*, December 19, 2021, forbes.com/sites/patrickhull/2012/12/19/be-visionary-think-big/?sh=17920fd33c17.

203 **"Truly great companies understand":** James C. Collins and Jerry I. Porras, "Building Your Company's Vision," *Harvard Business Review*, September–October 1996, cin.ufpe.br/~genesis/docpublicacoes/visao.pdf.

204 **Jeff Bezos put it more succinctly:** Adrien Beaulieu, "Inspiring Product Manager and Entrepreneurs Quotes—Series (1)," Product House, https://product.house/inspiring-product-manager-and-entrepreneurs-quotes-series-1-2/.

205 **Because I had the chance:** *PBD Podcast*, "Papa John | *PBD Podcast* | Ep. 184," YouTube video, September 14, 2022, youtube.com/watch?v=L-ItF79OHaU.

205 **It's no surprise that Papa John's:** "Papa John's Dominates the Pizza Category in Customer Satisfaction and Product Quality," Business Wire, June 20, 2017, businesswire.com/news/home/20170620006170/en/Papa-John%E2%80%99s-Dominates-the-Pizza-Category-in-Customer-Satisfaction-and-Product-Quality.

214 **Members of the club included:** Jordan Palmer, "At the Turn of the Century This Was Wealthy America's Most Coveted Vacation Destination," Travel Awaits, February 2, 2001, travelawaits.com/2561245/jekyll-island-coveted-vacation-history/.

215 **Almost half would consider quitting:** Paul Polman, "2023 Net Positive Employee Barometer: From Quiet Quitting to Conscious Quitting: How Companies' Values and Impact on the World Are Transforming Their Employee Appeal," paulpolman.com/wp-content/uploads/2023/02/MC_Paul-Polman_Net-Positive-Employee-Barometer_Final_web.pdf.

217 **Author Simon Sinek said:** Pat Heffernan, "People Don't Buy What You Do—They Buy WHY You Do It," Marketing Partners, October 7, 2010, https://www.marketing-partners.com/conversations2/people-dont-buy-what-you-do-they-buy-why-you-do-it.

228 **In Alex Banks's Twitter post:** Alex Banks (@thealexbanks), "Show your long-term vision..." Twitter, March 11, 2023, twitter.com/thealexbanks/status/1634547381122502659.

CHAPTER 11: ROLLING OUT THE PLAN

257 **Harvard Business School published:** Paul A. Gompers, William Gornall, Steven N. Kaplan, and Ilya A. Strebulaev, "How Do Venture Capitalists Make Decisions?" Harvard Business School, September 2016, https://www.hbs.edu/faculty/Pages/item.aspx?num=51659.